Letter to the Student

Sigmund Freud never wrote for SCIENTIFIC AMERICAN. During his lifetime, the magazine's focus tended much more toward technology and the natural sciences. But particularly after World War II, psychology and the other studies of human behavior grew explosively, with undeniable impact on society. Brilliant successors to Freud pushed forward with studies of the mind and its neurobiological underpinnings. Many of those great scientists, I am happy to say, did write for us.

This anthology presents a handful of their wonderful articles. Within the field of psychology, they are already regarded as classic, landmark papers. (Perhaps Elizabeth Loftus' article is too recent to have fully acquired that status, but I believe it soon will.) For decades, professionals and students alike have turned to these articles to read the scientific pioneers' own careful descriptions of their work.

Here we reprint those articles as they first appeared in SCIENTIFIC AMERICAN, along with introductions and study questions written by Peter Gray, so that modern readers can experience the original thrill of learning directly from the masters.

Sincerely,

JOHN RENNIE
EDITOR IN CHIEF
SCIENTIFIC AMERICAN

Nikolaas Tinbergen 1952

The Curious Behavior of the Stickleback

Relevant to Chapter 3, "Genetic and Evolutionary Foundations of Behavior."

In 1973, Nikolaas Tinbergen, Konrad Lorenz, and Karl von Frisch were awarded the Nobel Prize for their ground-breaking work in ethology. They were the first and to date the only people to win a Nobel Prize based purely on the study of behavior. In this classic *Scientific American* article you can read Tinbergen's own account of this famous study along with some of his other research aimed at understanding the stimuli and responses that make up the entire reproductive cycle of the stickleback, a little European freshwater fish. The article nicely illustrates the general methods and some of the most enduring findings of ethology. The general approach of ethology, along with specific examples of the findings of the early ethologists, is described in Chapter 3 of Gray's *Psychology*.

See pages 2 thru 6

STUDY QUESTIONS:

— Describe the sequence of behaviors that comprise the reproductive cycle of the stickleback fish.

— How did Tinbergen identify the sign stimulus for the male stickleback's attack response on invaders of his nesting territory?

— What did Tinbergen find to be the sign stimuli for (a) the male's zigzag courtship dance and (b) the female's laying of eggs?

— Under what conditions did Tinbergen observe "displacement activity" in sticklebacks, and how does he account for such behavior?

— How did Tinbergen show that the male's zigzag dance derives from a mix of two separate drives—aggression and sex?

— According to Tinbergen, how is the study of behavior in a relatively simple creature like the stickleback relevant to understanding the more complex and flexible behavior of mammals, including humans?

B. F. SKINNER 1951

How to Teach Animals

Relevant to Chapter 4, "Basic Processes of Learning."

The elements of operant conditioning are elegantly illustrated in this brief article by B. F. Skinner, the man who did the most to promote research on operant conditioning in psychology and to popularize it among nonpsychologists. The article is all at once an introduction to the basic concepts of operant conditioning and a practical guide to animal training. Skinner introduces the reader to such concepts as reinforcement, conditioned (or secondary) reinforcement, the value of immediate reinforcement, shaping

See pages 8 thru 11

of a response that is not already in the animal's repertoire, discrimination training, punishment, and inadvertent reinforcement of "annoying" behavior. Skinner repeatedly emphasizes his belief that success or failure in learning depends more upon the abilities of the trainer than upon the abilities of the learner. Skinner's belief in environmental determinism is further manifested in his statement, "When relevant conditions have been controlled, the behavior of the organism is fully determined." The article might be read most usefully before reading the more detailed discussion of operant conditioning in Chapter 4 of Gray's *Psychology*.

STUDY QUESTIONS:

— Describe Skinner's method for training a dog to perform some arbitrary response, such as touching a cupboard door with its nose. In such training, what is the function of the conditioned reinforcer?

— How can a pigeon be trained to (a) discriminate between hearts and clubs, (b) pick the card that matches the suit of any sample card, and (c) label the suit of any sample card?

— According to Skinner, how can the same basic procedures as those discussed for dogs and pigeons be applied in training a human infant to make a simple response, such as lifting its arm?

— Discuss Skinner's notion that we are almost always reinforcing or punishing the behavior of others, whether we want to or not.

— According to Skinner's analysis, how might parents' natural tendencies reinforce annoying behaviors in their children?

Michael Gazzaniga 1967

The Split Brain in Man

Relevant to Chapter 5, "The Nervous System."

In the 1960s Michael Gazzaniga began a series of research studies on patients who had undergone an operation in which the corpus callosum was sliced through to treat severe epilepsy. As a result of the operation, the right and left halves of the higher parts of these patients' brains could not communicate with each other. Through careful tests, Gazzaniga found that these patients seemed to have two separate minds, each capable of holding different information and each having strikingly different ways of dealing with that information. The finding was in some ways in line with the view of Sigmund Freud and other psychodynamic theorists, who had long contended that much goes on in the mind that people are unconscious of and unable to speak about. Gazzaniga's basic findings are summarized in Chapter 5 of Gray's *Psychology*, and they are elaborated upon more fully in this classic *Scientific American* article. This article, along with other writings by Gazzaniga, played a role in the cognitive revolution that occurred in psychology in the 1960s and 1970s, and in the conjoining of cognitive psychology with neuropsychology. His work illustrates a method of using behavioral observations to make inferences about the human mind, and a method of relating specific mental functions to specific anatomical portions of the brain.

See pages 12 thru 17

STUDY QUESTIONS:

— Explain in detail how Gazzaniga was able to send (a) visual and (b) tactile (touch) information selectively into the right or left hemisphere of split-brain patients.

— Explain how Gazzaniga was able to get information selectively *from* the left and right hemispheres of these patients. That is, how did he test left-hemisphere knowledge and abilities, and how did he test right-hemisphere knowledge and abilities?

— How did Gazzaniga and his colleagues show that the right hemisphere of some split-brain patients has some language ability?

— How did Gazzaniga and his colleagues show that the right hemisphere is better than the left at visual-constructional tasks?

— How did Young and Gazzaniga show that under some conditions a split-brain monkey can handle more visual information than normal monkeys can?

James Olds 1956

Pleasure Centers in the Brain

Relevant to Chapter 6, "Mechanisms of Motivation, Sleep, and Emotion."

I n the 1940s and 50s researchers first began to explore some of the behavioral functions of the brain by electrically stimulating deeply buried parts of the brain through thin wire electrodes. One of these pioneering researchers was James Olds, who discovered that animals will self-stimulate certain areas of their own brains very rapidly and persistently when they have the opportunity to do so. The activation of these brain areas is apparently highly rewarding, or pleasurable. In this classic *Scientific American* article, Olds presents his own account of the discovery of such "pleasure centers in the brain" and discusses some of the implications of the early experiments. As summarized in Chapter 6 of Gray's *Psychology*, Olds's initial discovery has led to much further research and to further understanding of the brain mechanisms of natural drives (such as hunger and thirst) and effects of abused drugs (such as cocaine).

See pages 19 thru 25

STUDY QUESTIONS:

— Why did the functional study of specific areas of the cerebral cortex precede, historically, the functional study of deep structures of the brain?

— How did Olds use W. R. Hess's method for stimulating brain areas?

— How did serendipity play a role in Olds's initial discovery of a reward area in the brain? In his initial studies, what led Olds to conclude that the electrical stimulation is rewarding?

— How did Olds use B. F. Skinner's method to quantify the rewarding effect of stimulating various parts of the brain, and what did he find using that method?

— What findings led Olds to suggest that there may be specialized reward areas for different drives, particularly for hunger and sex?

ELIZABETH F. LOFTUS 1997
Creating False Memories

Relevant to Chapter 9, "Memory."

Elizabeth Loftus, one of psychology's leading memory researchers, has focused her research primarily on questions about the creation of false and distorted memories. Her work has great practical significance, especially as applied to eyewitness memories in the courtroom and to memories constructed by patients in psychotherapy. In this article Loftus summarizes a

See pages 26 thru 31

number of experiments that demonstrate the roles of suggestion, social pressure, and imagination in the creation of false memories. Further discussion of the relation between original memories and constructed alterations of those memories can be found in Chapter 9 of Gray's *Psychology*.

STUDY QUESTIONS:

— How have court cases supported the concept that false memories, including rather fantastic false memories, can in some cases be constructed during psychotherapy?

— What is the "misinformation effect," and how has Loftus demonstrated it in laboratory experiments?

— How did Loftus and Pickrell demonstrate, in an experiment, that false childhood memories can be implanted in adults?

— How are imagination exercises sometimes used in police questioning and in therapists' offices to uncover lost memories? How have researchers shown that imagination exercises can promote the construction of false memories that are believed to be true?

— How did Nicholas Spanos and his colleagues implant "impossible memories" in people, concerning their first day after birth?

— In summary, describe the roles that the following play in the construction of false memories: (a) social demands; (b) imagination; (c) encouragement not to think about whether or not memory constructions are real; and (d) source confusion.

Eleanor Gibson & Richard Walk 1960
The "Visual Cliff"

Relevant to the chapter on perception,
and Chapter 11, "The Development of Thought and Language."

In this classic article, Eleanor Gibson and Richard Walk describe experiments in which they used a "visual cliff"—a drop-off underneath a transparent, thick sheet of glass—to test the depth perception and cliff avoidance of human babies and the young of various other species of animals. In one series of experiments they showed that the young of various species could perceive and avoid the cliff as soon as they were old enough to move about on their own—day one of life for chicks and kids (young goats) and about 6 to 8 months for human infants. These experiments subsequently inspired Joseph Campos and Bennett Bertenthal to study the role of self-produced locomotion in bringing on depth avoidance in human infants. In another series of experiments described in the *Scientific American* article, Gibson and Walk showed, with young rats and kittens, that early perception of the cliff depends much more on the cue of *motion parallax* than on the cue of *pattern density*. Further explanation of these cues for depth perception can be found in Gray's *Psychology*. (Note: The cue that Gibson and Walk refer to as *pattern density* is referred to by Gray as *texture gradient*.)

See pages 32 thru 39

STUDY QUESTIONS:

— What is the "visual cliff," and how is it used to assess depth perception in babies and young animals that are capable of moving on their own?

— At what age did (a) human infants, (b) chicks, (c) kids and lambs, and (d) kittens avoid the visual cliff?

— What general conclusions did Gibson and Walk draw from their comparisons of various species on the visual cliff, and how did they relate these conclusions to evolutionary theory?

— How did Gibson and Walk selectively abolish (a) the cue of pattern density and (b) the cue of motion parallax in studies with rats and other animals on the visual cliff?

— What specific findings led Gibson and Walk to suggest that the ability to assess depth based on motion parallax is innate, but the ability to assess depth based on pattern density may depend upon learning?

Harry Harlow 1959

Love in Infant Monkeys

Relevant to Chapter 12, "Social Development."

In the 1950s Harry Harlow initiated a series of experiments with infant rhesus monkeys that dramatically altered psychologists' conception of the nature of infants' attachments to their mothers. Up until that time many psychologists believed that an infant's drive to be with its mother (or other caretaker) is a secondary drive, conditioned through association of the mother with food. Harlow found that infant monkeys that were raised without a real monkey mother treated a cloth dummy as if it were a real mother and were comforted by the dummy's presence, whether or not the dummy was a source of food. The critical variable determining whether the dummy functioned as an effective mother for these purposes was not the provision of nutrition, but rather was the provision of contact comfort. The experiments are summarized briefly in Chapter 12 of Gray's *Psychology*, and on subsequent pages they are related to attachment in human infants. This classic *Scientific American* article presents, in Harlow's own words, a more complete description of the experiments and findings. Some people today question the ethics of these experiments, in which monkeys were raised in isolation from their mother or other real monkeys and suffered emotional consequences. Others counter that the experiments have furthered our understanding of the needs of infant humans (as well as monkeys) and have led to reforms in orphanages and to enlightened childrearing practices.

See pages 40 thru 46

STUDY QUESTIONS:

— According to Harlow, why are rhesus monkeys useful subjects for addressing questions about infant attachments in humans?

— Describe the experimental procedure and results that led Harlow to conclude that infants chose to spend much time clinging to the cloth surrogate, regardless of whether or not it was associated with nutrition.

— Describe the experiments and results that led Harlow to conclude that the presence of the cloth surrogate mother comforted infant monkeys in fearful situations and allowed them to explore a novel environment.

— What evidence led Harlow to conclude (a) that motion increases the effectiveness of a cloth surrogate mother and (b) that the act of clinging may play a role in the formation of attachment?

— What evidence led Harlow to suggest that maximal attachment to a surrogate mother does not occur if no surrogate is present during the first 8 months of the infant monkey's life?

Solomon Asch 1955

Opinions and Social Pressure

Relevant to Chapter 14, "Social Influences on Behavior."

Solomon Asch's experiments on conformity are among the most famous experiments in the history of psychology. They have been replicated around the world, almost always with similar results, and they have provoked much debate about human nature and social conditioning. When faced by a unanimous majority who gave the wrong response on a simple task of stating which of three lines was the same length as a fourth line, most of Asch's subjects denied the clear evidence of their own eyes, on at least some trials, and gave the same wrong response that the others had given. This *Scientific American* article was the route through which much of the intellectual world first heard of Asch's work. The article describes the basic experiment and several variations, including experiments varying the number of people in the unanimous majority, adding someone who gave the correct answer, and adding someone who gave an incorrect answer different from the majority. Asch's subsequent research, in which he tested the degree to which the social influence in this situation is primarily *normative* (based on the subject's desire to appear normal) or *informational* (based on the subject's desire to get the correct answer), as well as other follow-up research on conformity, is described in Chapter 14 of Gray's *Psychology*.

See pages 47 thru 51

STUDY QUESTIONS:

— What does Asch say about the history of psychological thought on conformity (or "suggestibility") preceding this research?

— Did the subjects in Asch's experiments submit easily and thoughtlessly to social pressure? Explain your answer. What reasons did they give for conforming or not conforming?

— In these experiments, what was the effect of (a) varying the number of people who unanimously chose the wrong line, and (b) adding a single person who chose the correct line?

— What was the effect of adding a dissenter who consistently chose an incorrect line that (a) was midway in length between the correct line and that chosen by the majority, or (b) was even more different in length from the correct line than was that chosen by the majority?

— What was the effect of adding a person who at first consistently chose the correct line and then began conforming with the majority? How did this differ from the effect of adding a person who consistently chose the correct line and then left the experiment?

The Curious Behavior of the Stickleback

This insignificant fish has a ceremonious sex life. To attract females the male builds a house, changes color and does a kind of dance, a ritual singularly useful to the study of instinct

by N. Tinbergen

WHEN I was a young lecturer in zoology at the University of Leyden 20 years ago, I was asked to organize a laboratory course in animal behavior for undergraduates. In my quest for animals that could be used for such a purpose, I remembered the sticklebacks I had been accustomed as a boy to catch in the ditches near my home and to raise in a backyard aquarium. It seemed that they might be ideal laboratory animals. They could be hauled in numbers out of almost every ditch; they were tame and hardy and small enough to thrive in a tank no larger than a hatbox.

I soon discovered that in choosing these former pets I had struck oil. They are so tame that they submit unfrightened to laboratory experiments, for the stickleback, like the hedgehog, depends on its spines for protection and is little disturbed by handling. Furthermore, the stickleback turned out to be an excellent subject for studying innate behavior, which it displays in some remarkably dramatic and intriguing ways. We found it to be the most reliable of various experimental animals that we worked with (including newts, bees, water insects and birds), and it became the focus of a program of research in which we now use hundreds of sticklebacks each year. The stickleback today is also a popular subject in various other zoological laboratories in Europe, notably at the universities in Groningen and Oxford. To us this little fish is what the rat is to many American psychologists.

My collaborator J. van Iersel and I have concentrated on the stickleback's courtship and reproductive behavior. The sex life of the three-spined stickleback (*Gasterosteus aculeatus*) is a complicated pattern, purely instinctive and automatic, which can be observed and manipulated almost at will.

In nature sticklebacks mate in early spring in shallow fresh waters. The mating cycle follows an unvarying ritual, which can be seen equally well in the natural habitat or in our tanks. First each male leaves the school of fish and stakes out a territory for itself, from which it will drive any intruder, male or female. Then it builds a nest. It digs a shallow pit in the sand bottom, carrying the sand away mouthful by mouthful. When this depression is about two inches square, it piles in a heap of weeds, preferably thread algae, coats the material with a sticky substance from its kidneys and shapes the weedy mass into a mound with its snout. It then bores a tunnel in the mound by wriggling through it. The tunnel, slightly shorter than an adult fish, is the nest.

Having finished the nest, the male suddenly changes color. Its normally inconspicuous gray coloring had already begun to show a faint pink blush on the chin and a greenish gloss on the back and in the eyes. Now the pink becomes a bright red and the back turns a bluish white.

IN THIS colorful, conspicuous dress the male at once begins to court females. They, in the meantime, have also become ready to mate: their bodies have grown shiny and bulky with 50 to 100 large eggs. Whenever a female enters the male's territory, he swims toward her in a series of zigzags—first a sideways turn away from her, then a quick movement toward her. After each advance the male stops for an instant and then performs another zigzag. This dance continues until the female takes notice and swims toward the male in a curious head-up posture. He then turns and swims rapidly toward the nest, and she follows. At the nest the male makes a series of rapid thrusts with his snout into the entrance. He turns on his side

as he does so and raises his dorsal spines toward his mate. Thereupon, with a few strong tail beats, she enters the nest and rests there, her head sticking out from one end and her tail from the other. The male now prods her tail base with rhythmic thrusts, and this causes her to lay her eggs. The whole courtship and egg-laying ritual takes only about one minute. As soon as she has laid her eggs, the female slips out of the nest. The male then glides in quickly to fertilize the clutch. After that he chases the female away and goes looking for another partner.

One male may escort three, four or even five females through the nest, fertilizing each patch of eggs in turn. Then his mating impulse subsides, his color darkens and he grows increasingly hostile to females. Now he guards the nest from predators and "fans" water over the eggs with his breast fins to enrich their supply of oxygen and help them to hatch. Each day the eggs need more oxygen and the fish spends more time ventilating them. The ventilating reaches a climax just before the eggs hatch. For a day or so after the young emerge the father keeps the brood together, pursuing each straggler and bringing it back in his mouth. Soon the young sticklebacks become independent and associate with the young of other broods.

TO GET light on the behavior of man, particularly his innate drives and conflicts, it is often helpful to study the elements of behavior in a simple animal. Here is a little fish that exhibits a complicated pattern of activities, all dependent on simple stimuli and drives. We have studied and analyzed its behavior by a large number of experiments, and have learned a good deal about why the stickleback behaves as it does.

Let us begin with the stimulus that

causes one stickleback to attack another. Early in our work we noticed that a male patrolling its territory would attack a red-colored intruder much more aggressively than a fish of some other color. Even a red mail van passing our windows at a distance of 100 yards could make the males in the tank charge its glass side in that direction. To investigate the reactions to colors we made a number of rough models of sticklebacks and painted some of the dummies red, some pale silver, some green. We rigged them up on thin wires and presented them one by one to the males in the tank. We found that the red models were always more provoking than the others, though even the silvery or green intruders caused some hostility.

In much the same way we tested the influence of shape, size, type of body movement and other stimuli, relating them to specific behavior in nest building, courting, attack, zigzag, fanning and so on. We discovered, for example, that a male swollen with food was courted as if it were a female.

As our work proceeded, we saw that the effective stimuli differed from one reaction to another, even when two reactions were caused by the same object. Thus a female will follow a red model wherever it leads; she will even make frantic efforts to enter a non-existent nest wherever the model is poked into the sand. Once she is in a real nest, she can be induced to spawn merely by prodding the base of her tail with a glass rod, even after she has seen the red fish that led her there removed. At one moment the male must give the visual signal of red; at the next, this stimulus is of no importance and only the tactile sensation counts. This observation led us to conclude that the stickleback responds simply to "sign stimuli," i.e., to a few characteristics of an object rather than to the object as a whole. A red fish or a red mail truck, a thrusting snout or a glass rod—it is the signal, not the object, that counts. A similar dependence on sign stimuli, which indicates the existence of special central nervous mechanisms, has been found in other species. It seems to be typical of innate behavior, and many social relationships in animals apparently are based on a system of signs.

Sticklebacks will respond to our stimuli only when they are in breeding condition. At other seasons they ignore the signs. This fact led us to investigate the internal factors that govern the fish. The obvious way to study such fluctuations is to measure the frequency and intensity of a response under standard stimulation. For some of these tests we used either uniform models or live fish confined in glass tubes so that we could control their movement. To measure the parental drive we adopted the standard of the number of seconds spent in fan-

MALE STICKLEBACK (*Gasterosteus aculeatus*) is photographed in full sexual markings. Its underside is a bright vermilion; its eyes, blue.

MALE STICKLEBACK DIGS in the sand after it has perceived its image in a mirror. This is one aspect of its behavior during a fight with another male.

IN FIRST STAGE of courtship the male stickleback (*left*) zigzags toward the female (*right*). The female then swims toward him with her head up. The abdomen of the female bulges with from 50 to 100 eggs.

IN SECOND STAGE, seen from above, the male stickleback swims toward the nest he has built and makes a series of thrusts into it with his snout. He also turns on his side and raises his dorsal spines toward the female.

ning a given number of eggs per time unit.

The stickleback's drives in the breeding sequence wax and wane in a series of cycles. Each drive runs its course in regular succession: first the male gets the urge to fight, then to build a nest, then to court a female, then to develop the brood. He will not start to build, even though material is available, until he has defended his territory for a while. Nor will he court until he has built the nest; females that approach him before the nest is finished are driven off or at best are greeted with a few zigzags. Within each cycle also there is a fixed rhythm and sequence; for example, if you fill up the pit the male has dug, he will dig one again before collecting nest material. After the pit has been filled several times, however, the fish will build the nest without completing the pit. The development of his inner drive overcomes outside interference.

It seems likely that the rise and fall of inner drives is controlled by hormonal changes, and we are now studying the effects on these drives of castrating and giving hormones to the males. One interesting finding so far is that castration abolishes the first phases of mating, but has no effect on the parental drive. A eunuch stickleback, when given a nest of eggs, ventilates it with abandon.

IN ANY animal the innate drives themselves are only the elementary forces of behavior. It is the interaction among those drives, giving rise to conflicts, that shapes the animal's actual be-

havior, and we have devoted a major part of our work with the stickleback to this subject. It struck us, as it has often struck observers of other animals, that the belligerent male sticklebacks spent little time in actual fighting. Much of their hostility consists of display. The threat display of male sticklebacks is of two types. When two males meet at the border of their territories, they begin a series of attacks and retreats. Each takes the offensive in his own territory, and the duel seesaws back and forth across the border. Neither fish touches the other; the two dart back and forth as though attached by an invisible thread. This behavior demonstrates that the tendency to attack and the tendency to retreat are both aroused in each fish.

When the fight grows in vigor, how-

IN THIRD STAGE, also seen from above, the female swims into the nest. The male then prods the base of her tail and causes her to lay her eggs. When the female leaves the nest, the male enters and fertilizes the eggs.

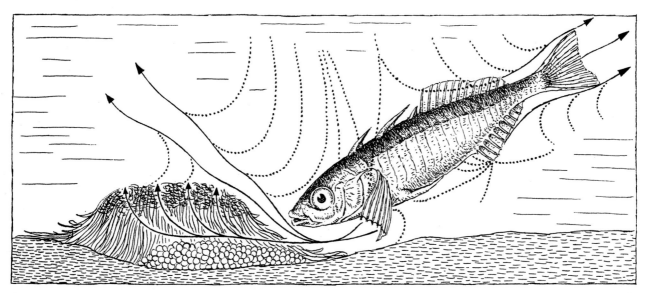

IN FOURTH STAGE the male "fans" water over the eggs to enrich their oxygen supply. The dotted lines show the movement of a colored solution placed in the tank; the solid lines, the direction of the water currents.

ever, the seesaw maneuver may suddenly change into something quite different. Each fish adopts an almost vertical head-down posture, turns its side to its opponent, raises its ventral spines and makes jerky movements with the whole body. Under crowded conditions, when territories are small and the fighting tendency is intense, both fish begin to dig into the sand, as if they were starting to build a nest! This observation at first astonished us. Digging is so irrelevant to the fighting stimulus that it seemed to overthrow all our ideas about the specific connection between sign and response. But it became less mysterious when we considered similar instances of incongruous behavior by other animals. Fighting starlings always preen themselves between bouts; in the midst of a fight roosters often peck at the ground as though feeding, and wading-birds assume a sleeping posture. Even a man, in situations of embarrassment, conflict or stress, will scratch himself behind the ear.

So it appears that the stickleback does not start digging because its nest-building drive is suddenly activated. Rather, the fish is engaging in what a psychologist would call a "displacement activity." Alternating between the urge to attack and to escape, neither of which it can carry out, it finally is driven by its tension to find an outlet in an irrelevant action.

THE THEORY of displacement activity has been tested by the following experiment. We place a red model in a male's territory and, when the fish attacks, beat it as hard as we can with its supposed antagonist. This unexpected behavior causes the fish to flee and hide in the weeds. From that shelter it glares at the intruder. Its flight impulse gradually subsides and its attack drive rises. After a few minutes the fish emerges from shelter and cautiously approaches the model. Then, just at the moment when attack and retreat are evenly balanced, it suddenly adopts the head-down posture.

A similar interaction of drives seems to motivate the male when he is courting. In the zigzag dance the movement away from the female is the purely sexual movement of leading; the movement toward her is an incipient attack. This duality can be proved by measur-

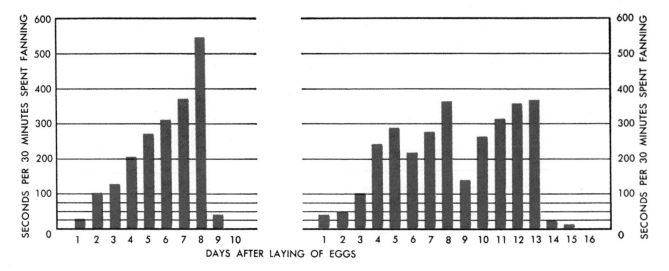

FANNING OF EGGS by the male stickleback follows a predictable pattern, as shown by the graph at the left. The fish spends more and more time fanning from the first day until the eighth. By the tenth day it has stopped fanning altogether. The graph at the right shows what happened when the eggs were removed on the sixth day and replaced with a fresh batch. The fanning pattern began anew, but the fanning time on the sixth day was still longer than that on the first. This suggested that fanning is controlled by internal as well as external factors.

ing the comparative intensity of the two drives in an individual male and relating it to his dance. Thus when the sex drive is strong (as measured by willingness to lead a standard female model) the zig component of the dance is pronounced and may shift to complete leading. When the fighting drive is strong (as measured by the number of bites aimed at a standard male model) the zag is more emphatic and may become a straightforward attack. A female evokes the double response because she provides sign stimuli for both aggression and sexuality. Every fish entering a male's territory evokes some degree of attack, and therefore even a big-bellied female must produce a hostile as well as a sexual response.

This complexity of drives continues when the fish have arrived at the nest. A close study of the movement by which the male indicates the entrance shows that it is very similar to fanning, at that moment an entirely irrelevant response. This fanning motion, we conclude, must be a displacement activity, caused by the fact that the male is not yet able to release his sex drive; he can ejaculate his sperm only after the female has laid her eggs. Even when the female has entered the nest, the male's drive is still frustrated. Before he can release it, he must stimulate her to spawn. The "quivering" motion with which he prods her is much like fanning. It, too, is a displacement activity and stops at the moment when the eggs are laid and the male can fertilize them. It is probable that the male's sex drive is frustrated not only by the absence of eggs but also by a strong conflict with the attack drive, which must be intense when a strange fish is so near the nest. This hostility is evident from the fact that the male raises his dorsal spines

while exhibiting the nest to the female.

The ideas briefly outlined here seem to throw considerable light on the complicated and "irrelevant" activities typical of innate behavior in various animals. Of course these ideas have to be checked in more cases. This is now being done, particularly with fish and birds, and the results are encouraging.

I AM often asked whether it is worth while to stick to one animal species for so long a time as we have been studying the stickleback. The question has two answers. I believe that one should not confine one's work entirely to a single species. No one who does can wholly avoid thinking that his animal is The Animal, the perfect representative of the whole animal kingdom. Yet the many years of work on the stickleback, tedious as much of it has been, has been highly rewarding. Without such prolonged study we could not have gained a general understanding of its entire behavior pattern. That, in turn, is essential for an insight into a number of important problems. For instance, the aggressive component in courtship could never have been detected by a study of courtship alone, but only by the simultaneous study of fighting and courtship. Displacement activities are important for an understanding of an animal's motivation. To recognize them, one must have studied the parts of the behavior from which they are "borrowed" as well as the drives which, when blocked, use them as outlets. Furthermore, the mere observation and description of the stickleback's movements has benefited from our long study. Observation improves remarkably when the same thing is seen again and again.

Concentration on the stickleback has

also been instructive to us because it meant turning away for a while from the traditional laboratory animals. A stickleback is different from a rat. Its behavior is much more purely innate and much more rigid. Because of its relative simplicity, it shows some phenomena more clearly than the behavior of any mammal can. The dependence on sign stimuli, the specificity of motivation, the interaction between two types of motivation with the resulting displacement activities are some of these phenomena.

Yet we also study other animals, because only by comparison can we find out what is of general significance and what is a special case. One result that is now beginning to emerge from the stickleback experiments is the realization that mammals are in many ways a rather exceptional group, specializing in "plastic" behavior. The simpler and more rigid behavior found in our fish seems to be the rule in most of the animal kingdom. Once one is aware of this, and aware also of the affinity of mammals to the lower vertebrates, one expects to find an innate base beneath the plastic behavior of mammals.

Thus the study of conflicting drives in so low an animal as the stickleback may throw light on human conflicts and the nature of neuroses. The part played by hostility in courtship, a phenomenon found not only in sticklebacks but in several birds, may well have a real bearing on human sex life. Even those who measure the value of a science by its immediate application to human affairs can learn some important lessons from the study of this insignificant little fish.

N. Tinbergen is lecturer in animal behavior at the University of Oxford.

SCIENTIFIC AMERICAN

Help Desk

For your convenience, we have summarized the answers to often-asked customer service questions and how to get in touch with us.

WWW.SCIAM.COM

Our award-winning internet resource, updated weekly and thoroughly linked to related sites. Here you will find timely and interesting current news, recent illustrated scientific articles, ask the editors, our on-line store, subscriptions, email, plus other features not found in *SCIENTIFIC AMERICAN,* and much more.

SCIENTIFIC AMERICAN

SCIENTIFIC AMERICAN is considered the authoritative source, keeping its readers up-to-date while enriching their world. Your subscription includes 12 monthly issues with in-depth Special Reports. Annual subscriptions: In U.S. $34.97. Elsewhere $55.

SCIENTIFIC AMERICAN EXPLORATIONS

Our new quarterly publication is a science resource for parents. Exciting and inspiring, it is a powerful tool parents and teachers can use to help children unlock the wonders of science and technology. Annual 4-issue subscription: In U.S. $15.80. Elsewhere $19.80. Call 800-285-5264 or visit the *Explorations* Web site at www.explorations.org

SCIENTIFIC AMERICAN FRONTIERS

The magazine's PBS television series, *Scientific American Frontiers*, is hosted by actor and life long science buff, Alan Alda. Beginning with the Fall 2000 broadcast season, there will be 10 one-hour episodes each season, with *Frontiers* becoming an integral part of a new PBS science programming initiative. Visit the *Scientific American Frontiers* Web site at www.pbs.org/saf

SUBSCRIPTION INQUIRIES

Call us: In the U.S. and Canada 1-800-333-1199. Elsewhere 1-515-247-7631. Email: subscriptions@sciam.com, or write: Subscription Manager; *Scientific American*; PO Box 3187; Harlan, IA 51537. You can locate the date of the last issue of your subscription on the mailing label. For changes of address, please notify us at least four weeks in advance, and include both old and new addresses.

ONLINE ARCHIVE

www.sciamarchive.com is an intuitive online knowledge base, with the complete contents of every issue of *Scientific American* published from 1993 through recent issues. Available for immediate access as platform-independent Adobe® Acrobat® (PDF) files. $5.00 for each article accessed. Searches are always free.

BACK ISSUES

In U.S. $9.95 each. Elsewhere $12.95 each. Many issues are available. Fax your order along with your Visa, MasterCard or American Express card information to: 1-212-355-0408.

REPRINTS

$4 each, minimum order is 10 copies, prepaid. Availability is limited. Write to: Reprint Department; Scientific American; 415 Madison Avenue; New York, NY 10017-1111; fax us at: 1-212-355-0408 or telephone 1-212- 451-8877.

PHOTOCOPYING RIGHTS

Granted by Scientific American, Inc., to libraries and others registered with the Copyright Clearance Center (CCC) to photocopy articles in this issue for the fee of $3.50 per copy of each article plus $0.50 per page. Such clearance does not extend to photocopying articles for promotion or other commercial purpose.

SCIENTIFIC AMERICAN

How to Teach Animals

Some simple techniques of the psychological laboratory can also be used in the home. They can train a dog to dance, a pigeon to play a toy piano and will illuminate the learning process in man

by B. F. Skinner

TEACHING, it is often said, is an art, but we have increasing reason to hope that it may eventually become a science. We have already discovered enough about the nature of learning to devise training techniques which are much more effective and give more reliable results than the rule-of-thumb methods of the past. Tested on animals, the new techniques have proved superior to traditional methods of professional animal trainers; they yield more remarkable results with much less effort.

It takes rather subtle laboratory conditions to test an animal's full learning capacity, but the reader will be surprised at how much he can accomplish even under informal circumstances at home. Since nearly everyone at some time or other has tried, or wished he knew how, to train a dog, a cat or some other animal, perhaps the most useful way to explain the learning process is to describe some simple experiments which the reader can perform himself.

"Catch your rabbit" is the first item in a well-known recipe for rabbit stew. Your first move, of course, is to choose an experimental subject. Any available animal—a cat, a dog, a pigeon, a mouse, a parrot, a chicken, a pig—will do. (Children or other members of your family may also be available, but it is suggested that you save them until you have had practice with less valuable material.) Suppose you choose a dog.

The second thing you will need is something your subject wants, say food. This serves as a reward—or to use a term which is less likely to be misunderstood—a "reinforcement" for the desired behavior. Many things besides food are reinforcing—for example, simply letting the dog out for a run—but food is usually the easiest to administer in the kind of experiment to be described here. If you use food, you must of course perform the experiment when the dog is hungry, perhaps just before his dinnertime.

The reinforcement gives you a means of control over the behavior of the animal. It rests on the simple principle that whenever something reinforces a particular activity of an organism, it increases the chances that the organism will repeat that behavior. This makes it possible to shape an animal's behavior almost as a sculptor shapes a lump of clay. There is, of course, nothing new in this principle. What is new is a better understanding of the conditions under which reinforcement works best.

To be effective a reinforcement must be given almost simultaneously with the desired behavior; a delay of even one second destroys much of the effect. This means that the offer of food in the usual way is likely to be ineffective; it is not fast enough. The best way to reinforce the behavior with the necessary speed is to use a "conditioned" reinforcer. This is a signal which the animal is conditioned to associate with food. The animal is always given food immediately after the signal, and the signal itself then becomes the reinforcer. The better the association between the two events, the better the result.

For the conditioned reinforcer you need a clear signal which can be given instantly and to which the subject is sure to respond. It may be a noise or a flash of light. A whistle is not effective because of the time it takes to draw a breath before blowing it. A visual signal like a wave of the arm may not always be seen by the animal. A convenient signal is a rap on a table with a small hard object or the noise of a high-pitched device such as a "cricket."

YOU are now ready to start the experiment with your dog. Work in a convenient place as free as possible from distraction. Let us say that you have chosen a "cricket" as your conditioned reinforcer. To build up the effect of the reinforcer begin by tossing a few scraps of food, one at a time and not oftener than once or twice a minute, where the dog may eat them. Use scraps of food so small that 30 or 40 will not greatly reduce the animal's hunger. As soon as the dog eats each scrap readily and without delay, begin to pair the cricket with the food. Sound the cricket and then toss a piece of food. Wait half a minute or so and repeat. Sound the cricket suddenly,

without any preparatory movements such as reaching for food.

At this stage your subject will probably show well-marked begging behavior. It may watch you intently, perhaps jump on you, and so on. You must break up this behavior, because it will interfere with other parts of the experiment. Never sound the cricket or give food when the dog is close to you or facing you. Wait until it turns away, then reinforce. Your conditioned reinforcer is working properly when your subject turns immediately and approaches the spot where it receives food. Test this several times. Wait until the dog is in a fairly unusual position, then sound the signal. Time spent in making sure the dog immediately approaches the food will later be saved manyfold.

Now, having established the noise as the reinforcer, you may begin teaching the dog. To get the feel of the technique start with some simple task, such as getting the dog to approach the handle on a low cupboard door and touch it with its nose. At first you reinforce any activity which would be part of the final completed act of approaching and touching the handle of the cupboard. The only permissible contact between you and the dog is *via* the cricket and the food. Do not touch the dog, talk to it, coax it, "draw its attention" or interfere in any other way with the experiment. If your subject just sits, you may have to begin by reinforcing any movement, however slight. As soon as the dog moves, sound the cricket and give food. Remember that your reaction time is important. Try to reinforce as nearly simultaneously with the movement as possible.

After your subject is moving freely about, reinforce any turn toward the cupboard. Almost immediately you will notice a change in its behavior. It will begin to face toward the cupboard most of the time. Then begin to reinforce only when the dog moves nearer the cupboard. (If you withhold reinforcement too long at this stage, you may lose the facing response. If so, go back and pick it up.) In a very short time—perhaps a minute or two—you should have the dog standing close to the cupboard. Now begin to pay attention to its head. Reinforce any movement that brings the nose close to the handle. You will have to make special efforts now to reduce the time between the movement and the reinforcement to the very minimum. Presently the dog will touch the handle with its nose, and after reinforcement it will repeat this behavior so long as it remains hungry.

Usually it takes no more than five minutes, even for a beginner, to teach a dog this behavior. Moreover, the dog does not have to be particularly smart to learn it; contrary to the usual view, all normal dogs will learn with about equal facility by this conditioning technique.

Before going on with other experiments test the effect of your conditioned reinforcer again two or three times. If the dog responds quickly and eats without delay you may safely continue. You should "extinguish" the response the dog has already learned, however, before teaching it another. Stop reinforcing the act of touching the cupboard handle until the dog abandons this activity.

As a second test, let us say, you want to teach the dog to lift its head in the air and turn around to the right. The general procedure is the same, but you may need some help in sharpening your observation of the behavior to be reinforced. As a guide to the height to which the dog's head is to be raised, sight some horizontal line on the wall across the room. Whenever the dog, in its random movements, lifts its head above this line, reinforce immediately. You will soon see the head rising above the line more and more frequently. Now raise your sights slightly and reinforce only when the dog's head rises above the new level. By a series of gradual steps you can get the dog to hold its head much higher than usual. After this you can begin to emphasize any turning movement in a clockwise direction while the head is high. Eventually the dog should execute a kind of dance step. If you use available food carefully, a single session should suffice for setting up this behavior.

HAVING tested your ability to produce these simple responses, you may feel confident enough to approach a more complex assignment. This time suppose you try working with a pigeon. Pigeons do not tame easily. You will probably want a cage to help control the bird, and for this you can rig up a large cardboard carton with a screen or lattice top and windows cut in the side for observing the bird. It is much less disturbing to the bird if you watch it from below its line of vision than if you peer at it from above. In general keep yourself out of the experimental situation as much as possible. You may still use a cricket as a conditioned reinforcer, and feed the bird by dropping a few grains of pigeon feed into a small dish through a hole in the wall. It may take several daily feedings to get the bird to eat readily and to respond quickly to the cricket.

Your assignment is to teach the pigeon to identify the visual patterns on playing cards. To begin with, hang a single card on a nail on the wall of the cage a few inches above the floor so that the pigeon can easily peck it. After you have trained the bird to peck the card by reinforcing the movements that lead to that end, change the card and again reinforce the peck. If you shuffle the cards and present them at random, the pigeon will learn to peck any card offered.

Now begin to teach it to discriminate among the cards. Let us say you are using diamonds and clubs (excluding face cards and aces) and want the bird to select diamonds. Reinforce only when the card presented is a diamond, never when it is a club. Almost immediately the bird will begin to show a preference for diamonds. You can speed up its progress toward complete rejection of clubs by discontinuing the experiment for a moment (a mild form of punishment) whenever it pecks a club. A good conditioned punishment is simply to turn off the light or cover or remove the card. After half a minute replace the card or turn on the light and continue the experiment. Under these conditions the response which is positively reinforced with food remains part of the repertoire of the bird, while the response that leads to a blackout quickly disappears.

There is an amusing variation of this

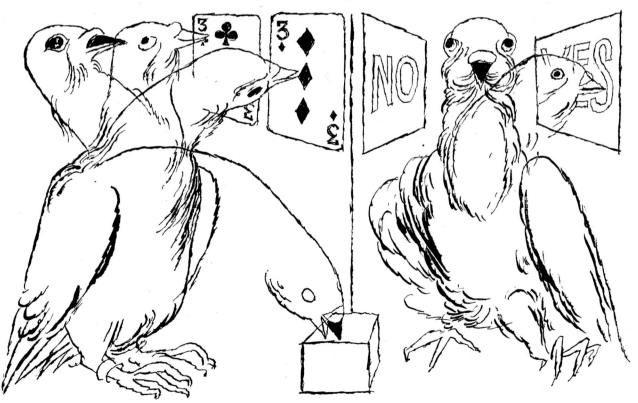

PIGEON can be taught to choose one card rather than another and even apparently to read. This is done by "reinforcing" the animal when it pecks the right card and turning out the light when it pecks the wrong one.

experiment by which you can make it appear that a pigeon can be taught to read. You simply use two printed cards bearing the words PECK and DON'T PECK, respectively. By reinforcing responses to PECK and blacking out when the bird pecks DON'T PECK, it is quite easy to train the bird to obey the commands on the cards.

The pigeon can also be taught the somewhat more "intellectual" performance of matching a sample object. Let us say the sample to be matched is a certain card. Fasten three cards to a board, with one above and the two others side by side just below it. The board is placed so that the bird can reach all the cards through windows cut in the side of the cage. After training the bird to peck a card of any kind impartially in all three positions, present the three chosen cards. The sample to be matched, say the three of diamonds, is at the top, and below it put a three of diamonds and a three of clubs. If the bird pecks the sample three of diamonds at the top, do nothing. If it pecks the matching three of diamonds below, reinforce it; if it pecks the three of clubs, black out. After each correct response and reinforcement, switch the positions of the two lower cards. The pigeon should soon match the sample each time. Conversely, it can also be taught to select the card that does not match the sample. It is important to reinforce correct choices immediately. Your own behavior must be letter-perfect if you are to expect

perfection from your subject. The task can be made easier if the pigeon is conditioned to peck the sample card before you begin to train it to match the sample.

IN A MORE elaborate variation of this experiment we have found it possible to make a pigeon choose among four words so that it appears to "name the suit" of the sample card. You prepare four cards about the size of small calling cards, each bearing in block letters the name of a suit: SPADES, HEARTS, DIAMONDS and CLUBS. Fasten these side by side in a row and teach the pigeon to peck them by reinforcing in the usual way. Now arrange a sample playing card just above them. Cover the name cards and reinforce the pigeon a few times for pecking the sample. Now present, say, the three of diamonds as the sample. When the pigeon pecks it, immediately uncover the name cards. If the pigeon pecks DIAMONDS, reinforce instantly. If it pecks a wrong name instead, black out for half a minute and then resume the experiment with the three of diamonds still in place and the name cards covered. After a correct choice, change the sample card to a different suit while the pigeon is eating. Always keep the names covered until the sample card has been pecked. Within a short time you should have the bird following the full sequence of pecking the sample and then the appropriate name card. As time passes the correct name will be pecked more and more frequently and, if you do not too

often reinforce wrong responses or neglect to reinforce right ones, the pigeon should soon become letter-perfect.

A toy piano offers interesting possibilities for performances of a more artistic nature. Reinforce any movement of the pigeon that leads toward its pressing a key. Then, by using reinforcements and blackouts appropriately, narrow the response to a given key. Then build up a two-note sequence by reinforcing only when the sequence has been completed and by blacking out when any other combination of keys is struck. The two-note sequence will quickly emerge. Other notes may then be added. Pigeons, chickens, small dogs and cats have been taught in this way to play tunes of four or five notes. The situation soon becomes too complicated, however, for the casual experimenter. You will find it difficult to control the tempo, and the reinforcing contingencies become very complex. The limit of such an experiment is determined as much by the experimenter's skill as by that of the animal. In the laboratory we have been able to provide assistance to the experimenter by setting up complicated devices which always reinforce consistently and avoid exhaustion of the experimenter's patience.

The increased precision of the laboratory also makes it possible to guarantee performance up to the point of almost complete certainty. When relevant conditions have been controlled, the behavior of the organism is fully determined. Behavior may be sustained in full

DOG can easily be trained to touch its nose to the handle of a cupboard with the aid of a mechanical "cricket."

The experimenter holds the cricket in one hand and a bit of food in the other. When the dog makes any move-

strength for many hours by utilizing different schedules of reinforcement. Some of these correspond to the contingencies established in industry in daily wages or in piece-work pay; others resemble the subtle but powerful contingencies of gambling devices, which are notorious for their ability to command sustained behavior.

THE human baby is an excellent subject in experiments of the kind described here. You will not need to interfere with feeding schedules or create any other state of deprivation, because the human infant can be reinforced by very trivial environmental events; it does not need such a reward as food. Almost any "feed-back" from the environment is reinforcing if it is not too intense. A crumpled newspaper, a pan and a spoon, or any convenient noisemaker quickly generates appropriate behavior, often amusing in its violence. The baby's rattle is based upon this principle.

One reinforcer to which babies often respond is the flashing on and off of a table lamp. Select some arbitrary response—for example, lifting the hand. Whenever the baby lifts its hand, flash the light. In a short time a well-defined response will be generated. (Human babies are just as "smart" as dogs or pigeons in this respect.) Incidentally, the baby will enjoy the experiment.

The same principle is at work in the behavior of older children and adults. Important among human reinforcements are those aspects of the behavior of others, often very subtle, that we call "attention," "approval" and "affection." Behavior which is successful in achieving these reinforcements may come to dominate the repertoire of the individual.

All this may be easily used—and just as easily misused—in our relations with other people. To the reader who is anxious to advance to the human subject a word of caution is in order. Reinforcement is only one of the procedures through which we alter behavior. To use it, we must build up some degree of deprivation or at least permit a deprivation to prevail which it is within our power to reduce. We must embark upon a program in which we sometimes apply relevant reinforcement and sometimes withhold it. In doing this, we are quite likely to generate emotional effects. Unfortunately the science of behavior is not yet as successful in controlling emotion as it is in shaping practical behavior.

A scientific analysis can, however, bring about a better understanding of personal relations. We are almost always reinforcing the behavior of others, whether we mean to or not. A familiar problem is that of the child who seems to take an almost pathological delight in annoying its parents. In many cases this is the result of conditioning which is very similar to the animal training we have discussed. The attention, approval and affection that a mother gives a child are all extremely powerful reinforcements. Any behavior of the child that produces these consequences is likely to be strengthened. The mother may unwittingly promote the very behavior she does not want. For example, when she is busy she is likely not to respond to a call or request made in a quiet tone of voice. She may answer the child only when it raises its voice. The average intensity of the child's vocal behavior therefore moves up to another level—precisely as the head of the dog in our experiment was raised to a new height. Eventually the mother gets used to this level and again reinforces only louder instances. This vicious circle brings about louder and louder behavior. The child's voice may also vary in intonation, and any change in the direction of unpleasantness is more likely to get the attention of the mother and is therefore strengthened. One might even say that "annoying" behavior is just that behavior which is especially effective in arousing another person to action. The mother behaves, in fact, as if she had been given the assignment to teach the child to be annoying! The remedy in such a case is simply for the mother to make sure that she responds with attention and affection to most if not all the responses of the child which are of acceptable intensity and tone of voice and that she never reinforces the annoying forms of behavior.

B. F. Skinner is professor of psychology at Harvard University.

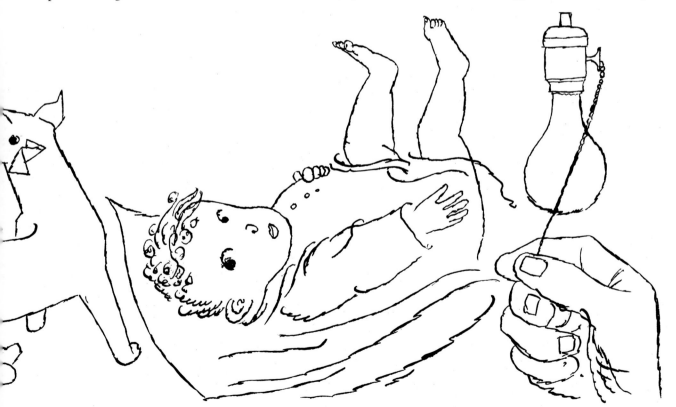

ment toward the handle, the experimenter sounds the cricket and tosses the food. Babies are just as smart as dogs in learning such tricks. At right a baby is taught to lift its arm when a lamp is turned off and on.

The Split Brain in Man

The human brain is actually two brains, each capable of advanced mental functions. When the cerebrum is divided surgically, it is as if the cranium contained two separate spheres of consciousness

by Michael S. Gazzaniga

The brain of the higher animals, including man, is a double organ, consisting of right and left hemispheres connected by an isthmus of nerve tissue called the corpus callosum. Some 15 years ago Ronald E. Myers and R. W. Sperry, then at the University of Chicago, made a surprising discovery: When this connection between the two halves of the cerebrum was cut, each hemisphere functioned independently as if it were a complete brain. The phenomenon was first investigated in a cat in which not only the brain but also the optic chiasm, the crossover of the optic nerves, was divided, so that visual information from the left eye was dispatched only to the left brain and information from the right eye only to the right brain. Working on a problem with one eye, the animal could respond normally and learn to perform a task; when that eye was covered and the same problem was presented to the other eye, the animal evinced no recognition of the problem and had to learn it again from the beginning with the other half of the brain.

The finding introduced entirely new questions in the study of brain mechanisms. Was the corpus callosum responsible for integration of the operations of the two cerebral hemispheres in the intact brain? Did it serve to keep each hemisphere informed about what was going on in the other? To put the question another way, would cutting the corpus callosum literally result in the right hand not knowing what the left was doing? To what extent were the two half-brains actually independent when they were separated? Could they have separate thoughts, even separate emotions?

Such questions have been pursued by Sperry and his co-workers in a wide-ranging series of animal studies at the California Institute of Technology over the past decade [see "The Great Cerebral Commissure," by R. W. Sperry; SCIENTIFIC AMERICAN, January, 1964]. Recently these questions have been investigated in human patients who underwent the brain-splitting operation for medical reasons. The demonstration in experimental animals that sectioning of the corpus callosum did not seriously impair mental faculties had encouraged surgeons to resort to this operation for people afflicted with uncontrollable epilepsy. The hope was to confine a seizure to one hemisphere. The operation proved to be remarkably successful; curiously there is an almost total elimination of all attacks, including unilateral ones. It is as if the intact callosum had served in these patients to facilitate seizure activity.

This article is a brief survey of investigations Sperry and I have carried out at Cal Tech over the past five years with some of these patients. The operations were performed by P. J. Vogel and J. E. Bogen of the California College of Medicine. Our studies date back to 1961, when the first patient, a 48-year-old war veteran, underwent the operation: cutting of the corpus callosum and other commissure structures connecting the two halves of the cerebral cortex [*see illustration on page 14*]. As of today 10 patients have had the operation, and we have examined four thoroughly over a long period with many tests.

From the beginning one of the most striking observations was that the operation produced no noticeable change in the patients' temperament, personality or general intelligence. In the first case the patient could not speak for 30 days after the operation, but he then recovered his speech. More typical was the third case: on awaking from the surgery the patient quipped that he had a "splitting headache," and in his still drowsy state he was able to repeat the tongue twister "Peter Piper picked a peck of pickled peppers."

Close observation, however, soon revealed some changes in the patients' everyday behavior. For example, it could be seen that in moving about and responding to sensory stimuli the patients favored the right side of the body, which is controlled by the dominant left half of the brain. For a considerable period after the operation the left side of the body rarely showed spontaneous activity, and the patient generally did not respond to stimulation of that side: when he brushed against something with his left side he did not notice that he had done so, and when an object was placed in his left hand he generally denied its presence.

More specific tests identified the main features of the bisected-brain syndrome. One of these tests examined responses to visual stimulation. While the patient fixed his gaze on a central point on a board, spots of light were flashed (for a tenth of a second) in a row across the board that spanned both the left and the right half of his visual field. The patient was asked to tell what he had seen. Each patient reported that lights had been flashed in the right half of the visual field. When lights were flashed only in the left half of the field, however, the patients generally denied having seen any lights. Since the right side of the visual field is normally projected to the left hemisphere of the brain and the left field to the right hemisphere, one might have concluded that in these patients with divided brains the right hemisphere was in effect blind. We found, however, that this was not the case when the patients were directed to point to the lights that had flashed instead of giving a verbal report. With this manual response they were able to indicate when lights had been flashed in the left visual field, and perception with the brain's right hemisphere proved to be almost equal to perception with the left. Clearly, then, the patients' failure to report the right hemisphere's perception verbally was due to the fact that the speech centers of the brain are located in the left hemisphere.

Our tests of the patients' ability to recognize objects by touch at first resulted in the same general finding. When the object was held in the right hand, from which sensory information is sent to the left hemisphere, the patient was able to name and describe the object. When it was held in the left hand (from which information goes primarily to the right hemisphere), the patient could not describe the object verbally but was able to identify it in a nonverbal test—matching it, for example, to the same object in a varied collection of things. We soon realized, however, that each hemisphere receives, in addition to the main input from the opposite side of the body, some input from the same side. This "ipsilateral" input is crude; it is apparently good mainly for "cuing in" the hemisphere as to the presence or absence of stimulation and relaying fairly gross information about the location of a stimulus on the surface of the body. It is unable, as a rule, to relay information concerning the qualitative nature of an object.

Tests of motor control in these split-brain patients revealed that the left hemisphere of the brain exercised normal control over the right hand but had less than full control of the left hand (for instance, it was poor at directing individual movements of the fingers). Similarly, the right hemisphere had full control of the left hand but not of the right hand. When the two hemispheres were in conflict, dictating different movements for the same hand, the hemisphere on the side opposite the hand generally took charge and overruled the orders of the side of the brain with the weaker control. In general the motor findings in the human patients were much the same as those in split-brain monkeys.

We come now to the main question on which we centered our studies, namely how the separation of the hemispheres affects the mental capacities of the human brain. For these psychological tests we used two different devices. One was visual: a picture or written information was flashed (for a tenth of a second) in either the right or the left visual field, so that the information was transmitted only to the left or to the right brain hemisphere [see illustration on page 27]. The other type of test was

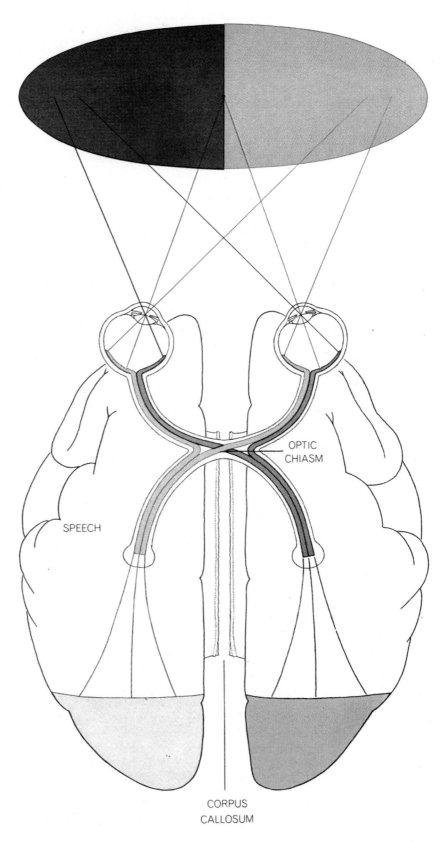

VISUAL INPUT to bisected brain was limited to one hemisphere by presenting information only in one visual field. The right and left fields of view are projected, via the optic chiasm, to the left and right hemispheres of the brain respectively. If a person fixes his gaze on a point, therefore, information to the left of the point goes only to the right hemisphere and information to the right of the point goes to the left hemisphere. Stimuli in the left visual field cannot be described by a split-brain patient because of the disconnection between the right hemisphere and the speech center, which is in the left hemisphere.

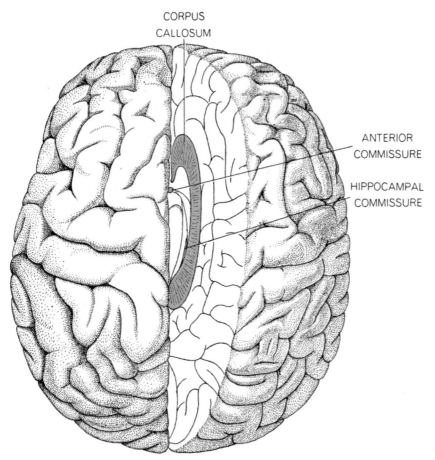

CORPUS
CALLOSUM

ANTERIOR
COMMISSURE

HIPPOCAMPAL
COMMISSURE

TWO HEMISPHERES of the human brain are divided by neurosurgeons to control epileptic seizures. In this top view of the brain the right hemisphere is retracted and the corpus callosum and other commissures, or connectors, that are generally cut are shown in color.

tactile: an object was placed out of view in the patient's right or left hand, again for the purpose of conveying the information to just one hemisphere—the hemisphere on the side opposite the hand.

When the information (visual or tactile) was presented to the dominant left hemisphere, the patients were able to deal with and describe it quite normally, both orally and in writing. For example, when a picture of a spoon was shown in the right visual field or a spoon was placed in the right hand, all the patients readily identified and described it. They were able to read out written messages and to perform problems in calculation that were presented to the left hemisphere.

In contrast, when the same information was presented to the right hemisphere, it failed to elicit such spoken or written responses. A picture transmitted to the right hemisphere evoked either a haphazard guess or no verbal response at all. Similarly, a pencil placed in the left hand (behind a screen that cut off vision) might be called a can opener or a cigarette lighter, or the patient might not

even attempt to describe it. The verbal guesses presumably came not from the right hemisphere but from the left, which had no perception of the object but might attempt to identify it from indirect clues.

Did this impotence of the right hemisphere mean that its surgical separation from the left had reduced its mental powers to an imbecilic level? The earlier tests of its nonverbal capacities suggested that this was almost certainly not so. Indeed, when we switched to asking for nonverbal answers to the visual and tactile information presented in our new psychological tests, the right hemisphere in several patients showed considerable capacity for accurate performance. For example, when a picture of a spoon was presented to the right hemisphere, the patients were able to feel around with the left hand among a varied group of objects (screened from sight) and select a spoon as a match for the picture. Furthermore, when they were shown a picture of a cigarette they succeeded in selecting an ashtray, from

a group of 10 objects that did not include a cigarette, as the article most closely related to the picture. Oddly enough, however, even after their correct response, and while they were holding the spoon or the ashtray in their left hand, they were unable to name or describe the object or the picture. Evidently the left hemisphere was completely divorced, in perception and knowledge, from the right.

Other tests showed that the right hemisphere did possess a certain amount of language comprehension. For example, when the word "pencil" was flashed to the right hemisphere, the patients were able to pick out a pencil from a group of unseen objects with the left hand. And when a patient held an object in the left hand (out of view), although he could not say its name or describe it, he was later able to point to a card on which the name of the object was written.

In one particularly interesting test the word "heart" was flashed across the center of the visual field, with the "he" portion to the left of the center and "art" to the right. Asked to tell what the word was, the patients would say they had seen "art"—the portion projected to the left brain hemisphere (which is responsible for speech). Curiously when, after "heart" had been flashed in the same way, the patients were asked to point with the left hand to one of two cards—"art" or "he"—to identify the word they had seen, they invariably pointed to "he." The experiment showed clearly that both hemispheres had simultaneously observed the portions of the word available to them and that in this particular case the right hemisphere, when it had had the opportunity to express itself, had prevailed over the left.

Because an auditory input to one ear goes to both sides of the brain, we conducted tests for the comprehension of words presented audibly to the right hemisphere not by trying to limit the original input but by limiting the ability to answer to the right hemisphere. This was done most easily by having a patient use his left hand to retrieve, from a grab bag held out of view, an object named by the examiner. We found that the patients could easily retrieve such objects as a watch, comb, marble or coin. The object to be retrieved did not even have to be named; it might simply be described or alluded to. For example, the command "Retrieve the fruit monkeys like best" results in the patients' pulling out a banana from a grab bag full of plastic fruit; at the command "Sunkist sells a lot of them" the patients retrieve an orange. We knew that touch information from the left hand was going exclusively to the right hemisphere because moments later, when the patients were asked to name various pieces of fruit placed in the left hand, they were unable to score above a chance level.

The upper limit of linguistic abilities in each hemisphere varies from subject to subject. In one case there was little or no evidence for language abilities in the right hemisphere, whereas in the other three the amount and extent of the capacities varied. The most adept patient showed some evidence of even being able to spell simple words by placing plastic letters on a table with his left hand. The subject was told to spell a word such as "pie," and the examiner then placed the three appropriate letters, one at a time in a random order, in his left hand to be arranged on the table. The patient was able to spell even more abstract words such as "how," "what" and "the." In another test three or four letters were placed in a pile, again out of view, to be felt with the left hand. The letters available in each trial would spell only one word, and the instructions to the subject were "Spell a word." The patient was able to spell such words as "cup" and "love." Yet after he had completed this task, the patient was unable to name the word he had just spelled!

The possibility that the right hemisphere has not only some language but even some speech capabilities cannot be ruled out, although at present there is no firm evidence for this. It would not be surprising to discover that the patients are capable of a few simple exclamatory remarks, particularly when under emotional stress. The possibility also remains, of course, that speech of some type could be trained into the right hemisphere. Tests aimed at this question, however, would have to be closely scrutinized and controlled.

The reason is that here, as in many of the tests, "cross-cuing" from one hemisphere to the other could be held responsible for any positive findings. We had a case of such cross-cuing during a series of tests of whether the right hemisphere could respond verbally to simple red or green stimuli. At first, after either a red or a green light was flashed to the right hemisphere, the patient would guess the color at a chance level, as might be expected if the speech mechanism is solely represented in the left hemisphere. After a few trials, however, the score improved whenever the examiner allowed a second guess.

We soon caught on to the strategy the patient used. If a red light was flashed and the patient by chance guessed red, he would stick with that answer. If the flashed light was red and the patient by chance guessed green, he would frown,

shake his head and then say, "Oh no, I meant red." What was happening was that the right hemisphere saw the red light and heard the left hemisphere make the guess "green." Knowing that the answer was wrong, the right hemisphere precipitated a frown and a shake of the head, which in turn cued in the left hemisphere to the fact that the answer was wrong and that it had better correct itself! We have learned that this cross-cuing mechanism can become extremely refined. The realization that the neurological patient has various strategies at his command emphasizes how difficult it is to obtain a clear neurological description of a human being with brain damage.

Is the language comprehension by the right hemisphere that the patients exhibited in these tests a normal capability of that hemisphere or was it acquired by learning after their operation, perhaps during the course of the experiments themselves? The issue is difficult to decide. We must remember that we are examining a half of the human brain, a system easily capable of learning from a single trial in a test. We do know that the right hemisphere is decidedly inferior to the left in its overall command of language. We have established, for instance, that although the right hemisphere can respond to a concrete noun such as "pencil," it cannot do as well with verbs; patients are unable to re-

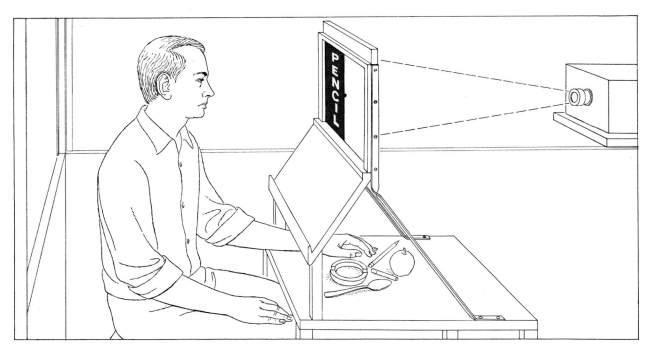

RESPONSE TO VISUAL STIMULUS is tested by flashing a word or a picture of an object on a translucent screen. The examiner first checks the subject's gaze to be sure it is fixed on a dot that marks the center of the visual field. The examiner may call for a verbal response—reading the flashed word, for example—or for a nonverbal one, such as picking up the object that is named from among a number of things spread on the table. The objects are hidden from the subject's view so that they can be identified only by touch.

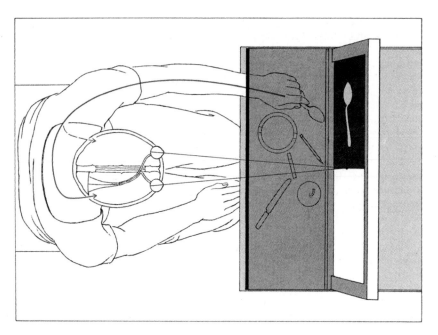

VISUAL-TACTILE ASSOCIATION is performed by a split-brain patient. A picture of a spoon is flashed to the right hemisphere; with the left hand he retrieves a spoon from behind the screen. The touch information from the left hand projects (*color*) mainly to the right hemisphere, but a weak "ipsilateral" component goes to the left hemisphere. This is usually not enough to enable him to say (using the left hemisphere) what he has picked up.

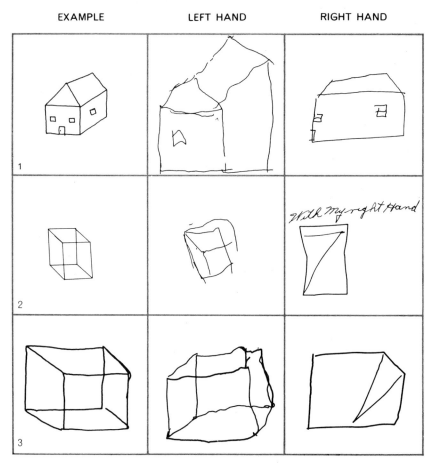

EXAMPLE	LEFT HAND	RIGHT HAND

"VISUAL-CONSTRUCTIONAL" tasks are handled better by the right hemisphere. This was seen most clearly in the first patient, who had poor ipsilateral control of his right hand. Although right-handed, he could copy the examples only with his left hand.

spond appropriately to simple printed instructions, such as "smile" or "frown," when these words are flashed to the right hemisphere, nor can they point to a picture that corresponds to a flashed verb. Some of our recent studies at the University of California at Santa Barbara also indicate that the right hemisphere has a very poorly developed grammar; it seems to be incapable of forming the plural of a given word, for example.

In general, then, the extent of language present in the adult right hemisphere in no way compares with that present in the left hemisphere or, for that matter, with the extent of language present in the child's right hemisphere. Up to the age of four or so, it would appear from a variety of neurological observations, the right hemisphere is about as proficient in handling language as the left. Moreover, studies of the child's development of language, particularly with respect to grammar, strongly suggest that the foundations of grammar—a ground plan for language, so to speak—are somehow inherent in the human organism and are fully realized between the ages of two and three. In other words, in the young child each hemisphere is about equally developed with respect to language and speech function. We are thus faced with the interesting question of why the right hemisphere at an early age and stage of development possesses substantial language capacity whereas at a more adult stage it possesses a rather poor capacity. It is difficult indeed to conceive of the underlying neurological mechanism that would allow for the establishment of a capacity of a high order in a particular hemisphere on a temporary basis. The implication is that during maturation the processes and systems active in making this capacity manifest are somehow inhibited and dismantled in the right hemisphere and allowed to reside only in the dominant left hemisphere.

Yet the right hemisphere is not in all respects inferior or subordinate to the left. Tests have demonstrated that it excels the left in some specialized functions. As an example, tests by us and by Bogen have shown that in these patients the left hand is capable of arranging blocks to match a pictured design and of drawing a cube in three dimensions, whereas the right hand, deprived of instructions from the right hemisphere, could not perform either of these tasks.

It is of interest to note, however, that although the patients (our first subject in particular) could not execute such tasks with the right hand, they were capable of matching a test stimulus to the correct design when it appeared among five related patterns presented in their right visual field. This showed that the dominant left hemisphere is capable of discriminating between correct and incorrect stimuli. Since it is also true that the patients have no motor problems with their right hand, the patients' inability to perform these tasks must reflect a break down of an integrative process somewhere between the sensory system and the motor system.

We found that in certain other mental processes the right hemisphere is on a par with the left. In particular, it can independently generate an emotional reaction. In one of our experiments exploring the matter we would present a series of ordinary objects and then suddenly flash a picture of a nude woman. This evoked an amused reaction regardless of whether the picture was presented to the left hemisphere or to the right. When the picture was flashed to the left hemisphere of a female patient, she laughed and verbally identified the picture as a nude. When it was later presented to the right hemisphere, she said in reply to a question that she saw nothing, but almost immediately a sly smile spread over her face and she began to chuckle. Asked what she was laughing at, she said: "I don't know...nothing...oh—that funny machine." Although the right hemisphere could not describe what it had seen, the sight nevertheless elicited an emotional response like the one evoked from the left hemisphere.

Taken together, our studies seem to demonstrate conclusively that in a split-brain situation we are really dealing with two brains, each separately capable of mental functions of a high order. This implies that the two brains should have twice as large a span of attention—that is, should be able to handle twice as much information—as a normal whole brain. We have not yet tested this precisely in human patients, but E. D. Young and I have found that a split-brain monkey can indeed deal with nearly twice as much information as a normal animal [see illustration below]. We have so far determined also that brain-bisected patients can carry out two tasks as fast as a normal person can do one.

Just how does the corpus callosum of the intact brain combine and integrate the perceptions and knowledge of the two cerebral hemispheres? This has been investigated recently by Giovanni Berlucchi, Giacomo Rizzolati and me at the Istituto di Fisiologia Umana in Pisa. We made recordings of neural activity in the posterior part of the callosum of the cat with the hope of relating the responses of that structure to stimulation of the animal's visual fields. The kinds of responses recorded turned out to be similar to those observed in the visual cortex of the cat. In other words, the results suggest that visual pattern information can be transmitted through the callosum. This finding militates against the notion that learning and memory are transferred across the callosum, as has usually been suggested. Instead, it looks as though in animals with an intact callosum a copy of the visual world as seen in one hemisphere is sent over to the other, with the result that both hemispheres can learn together a discrimination presented to just one hemisphere. In the split-brain animal this extension of the visual pathway is cut off; this would explain rather simply why no learning proceeds in the visually isolated hemisphere and why it has to learn the discrimination from scratch.

Curiously, however, the neural activity in the callosum came only in response to stimuli at the midline of the visual field. This finding raises difficult questions. How can it be reconciled with the well-established observation that the left hemisphere of a normal person can give a running description of all the visual information presented throughout the entire half-field projected to the right hemisphere? For this reason alone one is wearily driven back to the conclusion that somewhere and somehow all or part of the callosum transmits not only a visual scene but also a complicated neural code of a higher order.

All the evidence indicates that separation of the hemispheres creates two independent spheres of consciousness within a single cranium, that is to say, within a single organism. This conclusion is disturbing to some people who view consciousness as an indivisible property of the human brain. It seems premature to others, who insist that the capacities revealed thus far for the right hemisphere are at the level of an automaton. There is, to be sure, hemispheric inequality in the present cases, but it may well be a characteristic of the individuals we have studied. It is entirely possible that if a human brain were divided in a very young person, both hemispheres could as a result separately and independently develop mental functions of a high order at the level attained only in the left hemisphere of normal individuals.

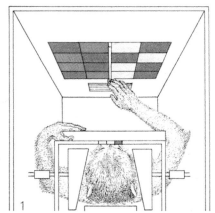 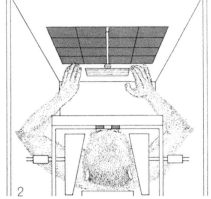 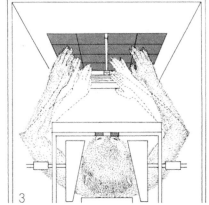

SPLIT-BRAIN MONKEYS can handle more visual information than normal animals. When the monkey pulls a knob (1), eight of the 16 panels light momentarily. The monkey must then start at the bottom and punch the lights that were lit and no others (2). With the panels lit for 600 milliseconds normal monkeys get up to the third row from the bottom before forgetting which panels were lit (3). Split-brain monkeys complete the entire task with the panels lit only 200 milliseconds. The monkeys look at the panels through filters; since the optic chiasm is cut in these animals, the filters allow each hemisphere to see the colored panels on one side only.

Pleasure Centers in the Brain

Rats can be made to gratify the drives of hunger, thirst and sex by self-stimulation of their brains with electricity. It appears that motivation, like sensation, has local centers in the brain

by James Olds

The brain has been mapped in various ways by modern physiologists. They have located the sensory and motor systems and the seats of many kinds of behavior—centers where messages of sight, sound, touch and action are received and interpreted. Where, then, dwell the "higher feelings," such as love, fear, pain and pleasure? Up to three years ago the notion that the emotions had specific seats in the brain might have been dismissed as naive—

akin perhaps to medieval anatomy or phrenology. But recent research has brought a surprising turn of affairs. The brain does seem to have definite loci of pleasure and pain, and we shall review here the experiments which have led to this conclusion.

The classical mapping exploration of the brain ranged mainly over its broad, fissured roof—the cortex—and there localized the sensory and motor systems and other areas which seemed to control

most overt behavior. Other areas of the brain remained mostly unexplored, and comparatively little was known about their functions. Particularly mysterious was the series of structures lying along the mid-line of the brain from the roof down to the spinal cord, structures which include the hypothalamus and parts of the thalamus [*see diagram on page 21*]. It was believed that general functions of the brain might reside in these structures. But they were difficult

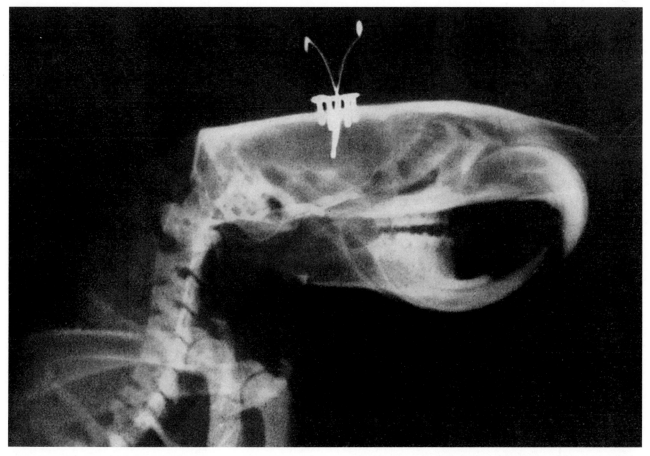

IMPLANTED ELECTRODES in the brain of a rat are shown in this X-ray photograph. The electrodes are held in a plastic carrier screwed to the skull. They can be used to give an electrical stimulus to the brain or to record electrical impulses generated by the brain.

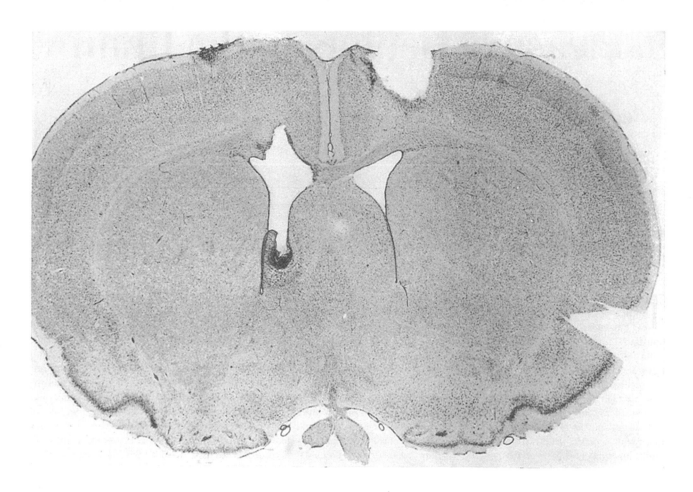

RAT'S BRAIN in a photomicrographic cross section shows a black spot to left of center, marking the point where electrical stimulus was applied. Such cross sections make it possible to tell exactly which center in the brain was involved in the animal's response.

to investigate, for two reasons. First, the structures were hard to get at. Most of them lie deep in the brain and could not be reached without damaging the brain, whereas the cortex could be explored by electrical stimulators and recording instruments touching the surface. Secondly, there was a lack of psychological tools for measuring the more general responses of an animal. It is easy to test an animal's reaction to stimulation of a motor center in the brain, for it takes the simple form of flexing a muscle, but how is one to measure an animal's feeling of pleasure?

The first difficulty was overcome by the development of an instrument for probing the brain. Basically the instrument is a very fine needle electrode which can be inserted to any point of the brain without damage. In the early experiments the brain of an animal could be probed only with some of its skull removed and while it was under anesthesia. But W. R. Hess in Zurich developed a method of studying the brain for longer periods and under more normal circumstances. The electrodes were inserted through the skull, fixed in position

and left there; after the skin healed over the wound, the animal could be studied in its ordinary activities.

Using the earlier technique, H. W. Magoun and his collaborators at Northwestern University explored the region known as the "reticular system" in the lower part of the mid-brain [see opposite page]. They showed that this system controls the sleep and wakefulness of animals. Stimulation of the system produced an "alert" electrical pattern, even from an anesthetized animal, and injury to nerve cells there produced more or less continuous sleep.

Hess, with his new technique, examined the hypothalamus and the region around the septum (the dividing membrane at the mid-line), which lie forward of the reticular system. He found that these parts of the brain play an important part in an animal's automatic protective behavior. In the rear section of the hypothalamus is a system which controls emergency responses that prepare the animal for fight or flight. Another system in the front part of the hypothalamus and in the septal area apparently controls rest, recovery, diges-

tion and elimination. In short, these studies seemed to localize the animal's brain responses in situations provoking fear, rage, escape or certain needs.

There remained an important part of the mid-line region of the brain which had not been explored and whose functions were still almost completely unknown. This area, comprising the upper portion of the middle system, seemed to be connected with smell, and to this day it is called the rhinencephalon, or "smell-brain." But the area appeared to receive messages from many organs of the body, and there were various other reasons to believe it was not concerned exclusively or even primarily with smell. As early as 1937 James W. Papez of Cornell University suggested that the rhinencephalon might control emotional experience and behavior. He based this speculation partly on the observation that rabies, which produces profound emotional upset, seems to attack parts of the rhinencephalon.

Such observations, then, constituted our knowledge of the areas of the brain until recently. Certain areas had been found to be involved in various kinds of emotional behavior, but the evidence was only of a general nature. The prevailing view still held that the basic motivations—pain, pleasure and so on—probably involved excitation or activity of the whole brain.

Investigation of these matters in more detail became possible only after psychologists had developed methods for detecting and measuring positive emotional behavior—pleasure and the satisfaction of specific "wants." It was B. F. Skinner, the Harvard University experimental psychologist, who produced the needed refinement. He worked out a technique for measuring the rewarding effect of a stimulus (or the degree of satisfaction) in terms of the frequency with which an animal would perform an act which led to the reward. For example, the animal was placed in a bare box containing a lever it could manipulate. If it received no reward when it pressed the lever, the animal might perform this act perhaps five to 10 times an hour. But if it was rewarded with a pellet of food every time it worked the lever, then its rate of performing the act would rise to 100 or more times per hour. This increase in response frequency from five or 10 to 100 per hour provided a measure of the rewarding effect of the food. Other stimuli produce different response rates, and in each case the rise in rate seems to be a quite accurate measure of the reward value of the given stimulus.

With the help of Hess's technique for probing the brain and Skinner's for measuring motivation, we have been engaged in a series of experiments which began three years ago under the guidance of the psychologist D. O. Hebb at McGill University. At the beginning we planned to explore particularly the midbrain reticular system—the sleep-control area that had been investigated by Magoun.

Just before we began our own work, H. R. Delgado, W. W. Roberts and N. E. Miller at Yale University had undertaken a similar study. They had located an area in the lower part of the mid-line system where stimulation caused the animal to avoid the behavior that provoked the electrical stimulus. We wished to investigate positive as well as negative effects—that is, to learn whether stimulation of some areas might be sought rather than avoided by the animal.

We were not at first concerned to hit very specific points in the brain, and in fact in our early tests the electrodes did not always go to the particular areas in

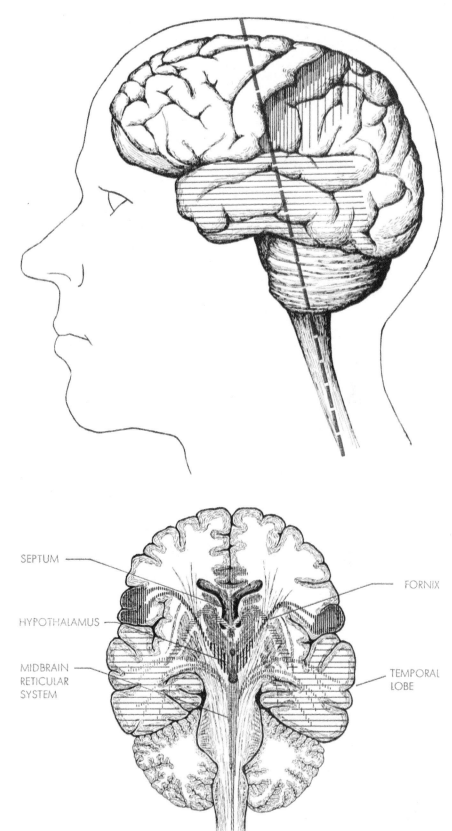

LOCATIONS OF FUNCTION in the human brain are mapped in these two diagrams. The white areas in both diagrams comprise the motor system; the black crosshatched areas, the sensory system. Crosshatched in color are the "nonspecific" regions now found to be involved in motivation of behavior. The diagram at bottom shows the brain from behind, dissected along the heavy dashed line at top. The labels here identify the centers which correspond to those investigated in the rat. The fornix and parts of the temporal lobes, plus associated structures not labeled, together constitute the rhinencephalon or "smell-brain."

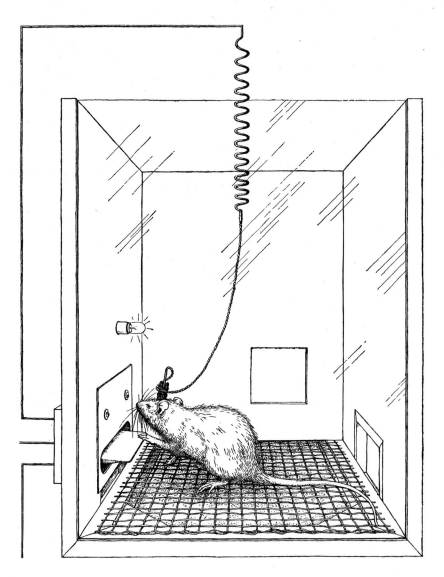

SELF-STIMULATION CIRCUIT is diagrammed here. When the rat presses on treadle it triggers an electric stimulus to its brain and simultaneously records action via wire at left.

the mid-line system at which they were aimed. Our lack of aim turned out to be a fortunate happening for us. In one animal the electrode missed its target and landed not in the mid-brain reticular system but in a nerve pathway from the rhinencephalon. This led to an unexpected discovery.

In the test experiment we were using, the animal was placed in a large box with corners labeled A, B, C and D. Whenever the animal went to corner A, its brain was given a mild electric shock by the experimenter. When the test was performed on the animal with the electrode in the rhinencephalic nerve, it kept returning to corner A. After several such returns on the first day, it finally went to a different place and fell asleep. The next day, however, it seemed even more interested in corner A.

At this point we assumed that the

stimulus must provoke curiosity; we did not yet think of it as a reward. Further experimentation on the same animal soon indicated, to our surprise, that its response to the stimulus was more than curiosity. On the second day, after the animal had acquired the habit of returning to corner A to be stimulated, we began trying to draw it away to corner B, giving it an electric shock whenever it took a step in that direction. Within a matter of five minutes the animal was in corner B. After this, the animal could be directed to almost any spot in the box at the will of the experimenter. Every step in the right direction was paid with a small shock; on arrival at the appointed place the animal received a longer series of shocks.

Next the animal was put on a T-shaped platform and stimulated if it turned right at the crossing of the T but not if it turned left. It soon learned to turn right every time. At this point we reversed the procedure, and the animal had to turn left in order to get a shock. With some guidance from the experimenter it eventually switched from the right to the left. We followed up with a test of the animal's response when it was hungry. Food was withheld for 24 hours. Then the animal was placed in a T both arms of which were baited with mash. The animal would receive the electric stimulus at a point halfway down the right arm. It learned to go there, and it always stopped at this point, never going on to the food at all!

After confirming this powerful effect of stimulation of brain areas by experiments with a series of animals, we set out to map the places in the brain where

such an effect could be obtained. We wanted to measure the strength of the effect in each place. Here Skinner's technique provided the means. By putting the animal in the "do-it-yourself" situation (*i.e.*, pressing a lever to stimulate its own brain) we could translate the animal's strength of "desire" into response frequency, which can be seen and measured.

The first animal in the Skinner box ended all doubts in our minds that electric stimulation applied to some parts of the brain could indeed provide reward for behavior. The test displayed the phenomenon in bold relief where anyone who wanted to look could see it. Left to itself in the apparatus, the animal (after about two to five minutes of learning) stimulated its own brain regularly about once every five seconds, taking a

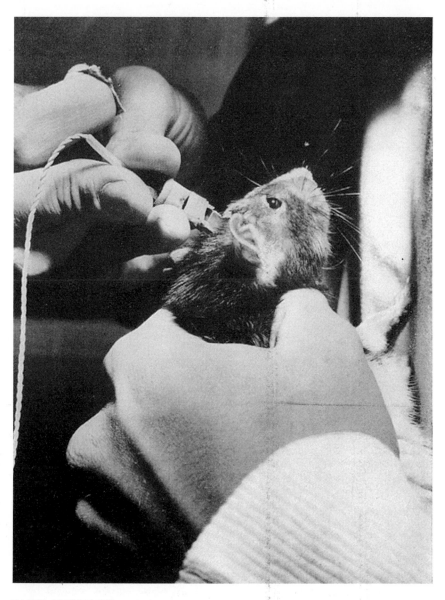

RAT IS CONNECTED to electrical circuit by a plug which can be disconnected to free the animal during rest periods. Presence of electrodes does not pain or discommode the rat.

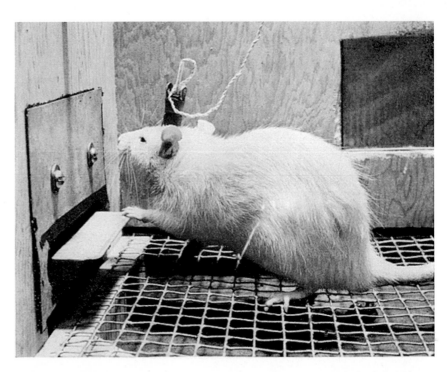

RAT SEEKS STIMULUS as it places its paw on the treadle. Some of the animals have been seen to stimulate themselves for 24 hours without rest and as often as 5,000 times an hour.

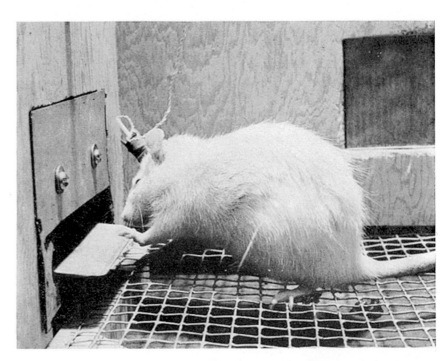

RAT FEELS STIMULUS as it presses on treadle. Pulse lasts less than a second; the current is less than .0005 ampere. The animal must release lever and press again to renew the stimulus.

stimulus of a second or so every time. After 30 minutes the experimenter turned off the current, so that the animal's pressing of the lever no longer stimulated the brain. Under these conditions the animal pressed it about seven times and then went to sleep. We found that the test was repeatable as often as we cared to apply it. When the current was turned on and the animal was given one shock as an *hors d'oeuvre*, it would begin stimulating its brain again. When the electricity was turned off, it would try a few times and then go to sleep.

The current used to stimulate was ordinary house current reduced by a small transformer and then regulated between one and five volts by means of a potentiometer (a radio volume control). As the resistance in the brain was approximately 12,000 ohms, the current ranged from about .000083 to .000420 of an ampere. The shock lasted up to about a second, and the animal had to release the lever and press again to get more.

We now started to localize and quantify the rewarding effect in the brain by planting electrodes in all parts of the brain in large numbers of rats. Each rat had a pair of electrodes consisting of insulated silver wires a hundredth of an inch in diameter. The two stimulating tips were only about one 500th of an inch apart. During a test the animal was placed in a Skinner box designed to produce a chance response rate of about 10 to 25 bar-presses per hour. Each animal was given about six hours of testing with the electric current turned on and one hour with the current off. All responses were recorded automatically, and the animal was given a score on the basis of the amount of time it spent stimulating its brain.

When electrodes were implanted in the classical sensory and motor systems, response rates stayed at the chance level of 10 to 25 an hour. In most parts of the mid-line system, the response rates rose to levels of from 200 to 5,000 an hour, definitely indicative of a rewarding effect of the electric stimulus. But in some of the lower parts of the mid-line system there was an opposite effect: the animal would press the lever once and never go back. This indicated a punishing effect in those areas. They appeared to be the same areas where Delgado, Roberts and Miller at Yale also had discovered the avoidance effect—and where Hess and others had found responses of rage and escape.

The animals seemed to experience the strongest reward, or pleasure, from stimulation of areas of the hypothalamus and certain mid-brain nuclei—regions which Hess and others had found to be centers for control of digestive, sexual, excretory and similar processes. Animals with electrodes in these areas would stimulate themselves from 500 to 5,000 times per hour. In the rhinencephalon the effects were milder, producing self-stimulation at rates around 200 times per hour.

Electric stimulation in some of these regions actually appeared to be far more rewarding to the animals than an ordinary satisfier such as food. For example, hungry rats ran faster to reach an electric stimulator than they did to reach food. Indeed, a hungry animal often ignored available food in favor of the pleasure of stimulating itself elec-

trically. Some rats with electrodes in these places stimulated their brains more than 2,000 times per hour for 24 consecutive hours!

Why is the electric stimulation so rewarding? We are currently exploring this question, working on the hypothesis that brain stimulation in these regions must excite some of the nerve cells that would be excited by satisfaction of the basic drives—hunger, sex, thirst and so forth. We have looked to see whether some parts of the "reward system" of the brain are specialized; that is, there may be one part for the hunger drive, another for the sex drive, etc.

In experiments on hunger, we have found that an animal's appetite for electric stimulation in some brain regions increases as hunger increases: the animal will respond much faster when hungry than when full. We are performing similar tests in other places in the brain with variations of thirst and sex hormones. We have already found that there are areas where the rewarding effects of a brain stimulus can be abolished by castration and restored by injections of testosterone.

Our present tentative conclusion is that emotional and motivational mechanisms can indeed be localized in the brain; that certain portions of the brain are sensitive to each of the basic drives. Strong electrical stimulation of these areas seems to be even more satisfying than the usual rewards of food, etc. This finding contradicts the long-held theory that strong excitation in the brain means punishment. In some areas of the brain it means reward.

The main question for future research is to determine how the excited "reward" cells act upon the specific sensory-motor systems to intensify the rewarded behavior.

At the moment we are using the self-stimulating technique to learn whether drugs will selectively affect the various motivational centers of the brain. We hope, for example, that we may eventually find one drug that will raise or lower thresholds in the hunger system, another for the sex-drive system, and so forth. Such drugs would allow control of psychological disorders caused by surfeits or deficits in motivational conditions.

Enough of the brain-stimulating work has been repeated on monkeys by J. V. Brady and J. C. Lilly (who work in different laboratories in Washington, D. C.) to indicate that our general conclusions can very likely be generalized eventually to human beings—with modifications, of course.

Creating False Memories

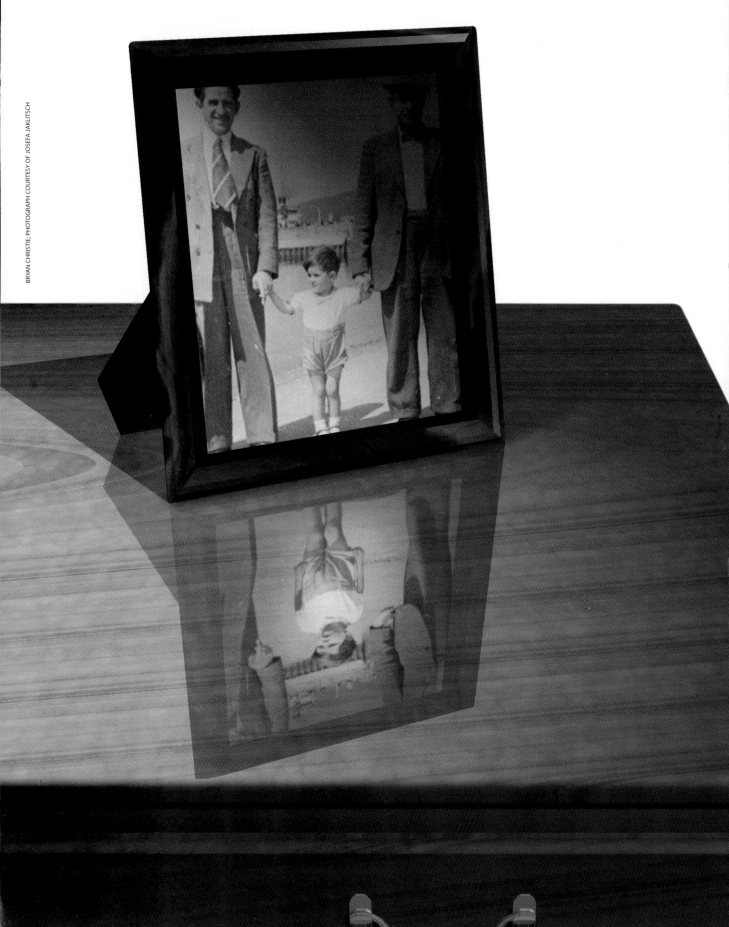

Researchers are showing how suggestion and imagination can create "memories" of events that did not actually occur

by Elizabeth F. Loftus

In 1986 Nadean Cool, a nurse's aide in Wisconsin, sought therapy from a psychiatrist to help her cope with her reaction to a traumatic event experienced by her daughter. During therapy, the psychiatrist used hypnosis and other suggestive techniques to dig out buried memories of abuse that Cool herself had allegedly experienced. In the process, Cool became convinced that she had repressed memories of having been in a satanic cult, of eating babies, of being raped, of having sex with animals and of being forced to watch the murder of her eight-year-old friend. She came to believe that she had more than 120 personalities—children, adults, angels and even a duck—all because, Cool was told, she had experienced severe childhood sexual and physical abuse. The psychiatrist also performed exorcisms on her, one of which lasted for five hours and included the sprinkling of holy water and screams for Satan to leave Cool's body.

When Cool finally realized that false memories had been planted, she sued the psychiatrist for malpractice. In March 1997, after five weeks of trial, her case was settled out of court for $2.4 million.

Nadean Cool is not the only patient to develop false memories as a result of questionable therapy. In Missouri in 1992 a church counselor helped Beth Rutherford to remember during therapy that her father, a clergyman, had regularly raped her between the ages of seven and 14 and that her mother sometimes helped him by holding her down. Under her therapist's guidance, Rutherford developed memories of her father twice impregnating her and forcing her to abort the fetus herself with a coat hanger. The father

had to resign from his post as a clergyman when the allegations were made public. Later medical examination of the daughter revealed, however, that she was still a virgin at age 22 and had never been pregnant. The daughter sued the therapist and received a $1-million settlement in 1996.

About a year earlier two juries returned verdicts against a Minnesota psychiatrist accused of planting false memories by former patients Vynnette Hamanne and Elizabeth Carlson, who under hypnosis and sodium amytal, and after being fed misinformation about the workings of memory, had come to remember horrific abuse by family members. The juries awarded Hammane $2.67 million and Carlson $2.5 million for their ordeals.

In all four cases, the women developed memories about childhood abuse in therapy and then later denied their authenticity. How can we determine if memories of childhood abuse are true or false? Without corroboration, it is very difficult to differentiate between false memories and true ones. Also, in these cases, some memories were contrary to physical evidence, such as explicit and detailed recollections of rape and abortion when medical examination confirmed virginity. How is it possible for people to acquire elaborate and confident false memories? A growing number of investigations demonstrate that under the right circumstances false memories can be instilled rather easily in some people.

My own research into memory distortion goes back to the early 1970s, when I began studies of the "misinformation effect." These studies show that when people who witness an event are later exposed to new and misleading information about it, their recollections often become distorted. In one example, participants viewed a simulated automobile accident at an intersection with

a stop sign. After the viewing, half the participants received a suggestion that the traffic sign was a yield sign. When asked later what traffic sign they remembered seeing at the intersection, those who had been given the suggestion tended to claim that they had seen a yield sign. Those who had not received the phony information were much more accurate in their recollection of the traffic sign.

My students and I have now conducted more than 200 experiments involving over 20,000 individuals that document how exposure to misinformation induces memory distortion. In these studies, people "recalled" a conspicuous barn in a bucolic scene that contained no buildings at all, broken glass and tape recorders that were not in the scenes they viewed, a white instead of a blue vehicle in a crime scene, and Minnie Mouse when they actually saw Mickey Mouse. Taken together, these studies show that misinformation can change an individual's recollection in predictable and sometimes very powerful ways.

Misinformation has the potential for invading our memories when we talk to other people, when we are suggestively interrogated or when we read or view media coverage about some event that we may have experienced ourselves. After more than two decades of exploring the power of misinformation, researchers have learned a great deal about the conditions that make people susceptible to memory modification. Memories are more easily modified, for instance, when the passage of time allows the original memory to fade.

False Childhood Memories

It is one thing to change a detail or two in an otherwise intact memory but quite another to plant a false memory of an event that never happened. To study false memory, my students and I

FALSE MEMORIES are often created by combining actual memories with suggestions received from others. The memory of a happy childhood outing to the beach with father and grandfather, for instance, can be distorted by a suggestion, perhaps from a relative, into a memory of being afraid or lost. False memories also can be induced when a person is encouraged to imagine experiencing specific events without worrying about whether they really happened or not.

first had to find a way to plant a pseudo-memory that would not cause our subjects undue emotional stress, either in the process of creating the false memory or when we revealed that they had been intentionally deceived. Yet we wanted to try to plant a memory that would be at least mildly traumatic, had the experience actually happened.

My research associate, Jacqueline E. Pickrell, and I settled on trying to plant a specific memory of being lost in a shopping mall or large department store at about the age of five. Here's how we did it. We asked our subjects, 24 individuals ranging in age from 18 to 53, to try to remember childhood events that had been recounted to us by a parent, an older sibling or another close relative. We prepared a booklet for each participant containing one-paragraph stories about three events that had actually happened to him or her and one that had not. We constructed the false event using information about a plausible shopping trip provided by a relative, who also verified that the participant had not in fact been lost at about the age of five. The lost-in-the-mall scenario included the following elements: lost for an extended period, crying, aid and comfort by an elderly woman and, finally, reunion with the family.

After reading each story in the book-let, the participants wrote what they remembered about the event. If they did not remember it, they were instructed to write, "I do not remember this." In two follow-up interviews, we told the participants that we were interested in examining how much detail they could remember and how their memories compared with those of their relative. The event paragraphs were not read to them verbatim, but rather parts were provided as retrieval cues. The participants recalled something about 49 of the 72 true events (68 percent) immediately after the initial reading of the booklet and also in each of the two follow-up interviews. After reading the booklet, seven of the 24 participants (29 percent) remembered either partially or fully the false event constructed for them, and in the two follow-up interviews six participants (25 percent) continued to claim that they remembered the fictitious event. Statistically, there were some differences between the true memories and the false ones: participants used more words to describe the true memories, and they rated the true memories as being somewhat more clear. But if an onlooker

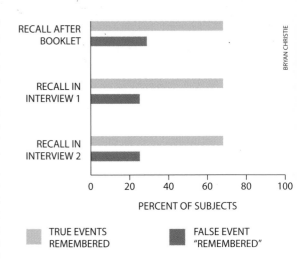

were to observe many of our participants describe an event, it would be difficult indeed to tell whether the account was of a true or a false memory.

Of course, being lost, however frightening, is not the same as being abused. But the lost-in-the-mall study is not about real experiences of being lost; it is about planting false memories of being lost. The paradigm shows a way of instilling false memories and takes a step toward allowing us to understand how this might happen in real-world settings. Moreover, the study provides evidence that people can be led to remember their past in different ways, and they can

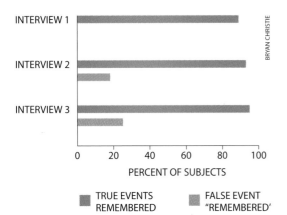

RECALL OF PLANTED CHILDHOOD EVENTS in this study appears to increase slightly after the details become familiar to the subject and the source of the information is forgotten. Ira Hyman and his colleagues at Western Washington University presented subjects with true events provided by relatives along with a false event—such as spilling a punch bowl on the parents of the bride at a wedding. None of the participants remembered the false event when first told about it, but in two follow-up interviews, initially 18 percent and later 25 percent of the subjects said they remembered something about the incident.

FALSE MEMORY TOOK ROOT in roughly 25 percent of the subjects in this study by the author and her co-workers. The study was designed to create a false recollection of being lost at age five on a shopping trip. A booklet prepared for each participant included the false event and three events that he or she had actually experienced. After reading the scenarios, 29 percent of the subjects "recalled" something about being lost in the mall. Follow-up interviews showed there was little variation over time in recalling both the false and true events.

even be coaxed into "remembering" entire events that never happened.

Studies in other laboratories using a similar experimental procedure have produced similar results. For instance, Ira Hyman, Troy H. Husband and F. James Billing of Western Washington University asked college students to recall childhood experiences that had been recounted by their parents. The researchers told the students that the study was about how people remember shared experiences differently. In addition to actual events reported by parents, each participant was given one false event—either an overnight hospitalization for a high fever and a possible ear infection, or a birthday party with pizza and a clown—that supposedly happened at about the age of five. The parents confirmed that neither of these events actually took place.

Hyman found that students fully or partially recalled 84 percent of the true events in the first interview and 88 percent in the second interview. None of the participants recalled the false event during the first interview, but 20 percent said they remembered something about the false event in the second interview. One participant who had been exposed to the emergency hospitalization story later remembered a male doctor, a female nurse and a friend from church who came to visit at the hospital.

In another study, along with true events Hyman presented different false events, such as accidentally spilling a bowl of punch on the parents of the bride at a wedding reception or having to evacuate a grocery store when the overhead sprinkler systems erroneously activated. Again, none of the participants recalled the false event during the first interview, but 18 percent remembered something about it in the second interview and 25 percent in the third interview. For example, during the first interview, one participant, when asked about the fictitious wedding event, stated, "I have no clue. I have never heard that one before." In the second interview, the participant said, "It was an outdoor wedding, and I think we were running around and knocked something over like the punch bowl or something and made a big mess and of course got yelled at for it."

Imagination Inflation

The finding that an external suggestion can lead to the construction of false childhood memories helps us understand the process by which false memories arise. It is natural to wonder whether this research is applicable in real situations such as being interrogated by law officers or in psychotherapy. Although strong suggestion may not routinely occur in police questioning or therapy, suggestion in the form of an imagination exercise sometimes does. For instance, when trying to obtain a confession, law officers may ask a suspect to imagine having participated in a criminal act. Some mental health professionals encourage patients to imagine childhood events as a way of recovering supposedly hidden memories.

Surveys of clinical psychologists reveal that 11 percent instruct their clients to "let the imagination run wild," and 22 percent tell their clients to "give free rein to the imagination." Therapist Wendy Maltz, author of a popular book on childhood sexual abuse, advocates telling the patient: "Spend time imagin-

JASON GOLTZ

ing that you were sexually abused, without worrying about accuracy, proving anything, or having your ideas make sense.... Ask yourself...these questions: What time of day is it? Where are you? Indoors or outdoors? What kind of things are happening? Is there one or more person with you?" Maltz further recommends that therapists continue to ask questions such as "Who would have been likely perpetrators? When were you most vulnerable to sexual abuse in your life?"

The increasing use of such imagination exercises led me and several colleagues to wonder about their consequences. What happens when people imagine childhood experiences that did not happen to them? Does imagining a childhood event increase confidence that it occurred? To explore this, we designed a three-stage procedure. We first asked individuals to indicate the likelihood that certain events happened to them during their childhood. The list contains 40 events, each rated on a scale ranging from "definitely did not happen" to "definitely did happen." Two weeks later we asked the participants to imagine that they had experienced some of these events. Different subjects were asked to imagine different events. Sometime later the participants again were asked to respond to the original list of

40 childhood events, indicating how likely it was that these events actually happened to them.

Consider one of the imagination exercises. Participants are told to imagine playing inside at home after school, hearing a strange noise outside, running toward the window, tripping, falling, reaching out and breaking the window with their hand. In addition, we asked participants questions such as "What did you trip on? How did you feel?"

In one study 24 percent of the participants who imagined the broken-window scenario later reported an increase in confidence that the event had occurred, whereas only 12 percent of those who were not asked to imagine the incident reported an increase in the likelihood that it had taken place. We found this "imagination inflation" effect in each of the eight events that participants were asked to imagine. A number of possible explanations come to mind. An obvious one is that an act of imagination simply makes the event seem more familiar and that familiarity is mistakenly related to childhood memories rather than to the act of imagination. Such source confusion—when a person does not remember the source of information—can be especially acute for the distant experiences of childhood.

Studies by Lyn Goff and Henry L. Roediger III of Washington University of recent rather than childhood experiences more directly connect imagined actions to the construction of false memory. During the initial session, the researchers instructed participants to perform the stated action, imagine doing it or just listen to the statement and do nothing else. The actions were simple ones: knock on the table, lift the stapler, break the toothpick, cross your fingers,

roll your eyes. During the second session, the participants were asked to imagine some of the actions that they had not previously performed. During the final session, they answered questions about what actions they actually performed during the initial session. The investigators found that the more times participants imagined an unperformed action, the more likely they were to remember having performed it.

Impossible Memories

It is highly unlikely that an adult can recall genuine episodic memories from the first year of life, in part because the hippocampus, which plays a key role in the creation of memories, has not matured enough to form and store long-lasting memories that can be retrieved in adulthood. A procedure for planting "impossible" memories about experiences that occur shortly after birth has been developed by the late Nicholas Spanos and his collaborators at Carleton University. Individuals are led to believe that they have well-coordinated eye movements and visual exploration skills probably because they were born in hospitals that hung swinging, colored mobiles over infant cribs. To confirm whether they had such an experience, half the participants are hypnotized, age-regressed to the day after birth and asked what they remembered. The other half of the group participates in a "guided mnemonic restructuring" procedure that uses age regression as well as active encouragement to re-create the infant experiences by imagining them.

Spanos and his co-workers found that the vast majority of their subjects were susceptible to these memory-planting procedures. Both the hypnotic and guided participants reported infant memories. Surprisingly, the guided group did so somewhat more (95 versus 70 percent). Both groups remembered the colored mobile at a relatively high rate (56 percent of the guided group and 46 percent of the hypnotic subjects). Many participants who did not remember the

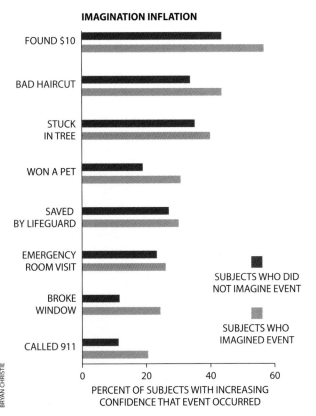

IMAGINATION INFLATION

FOUND $10
BAD HAIRCUT
STUCK IN TREE
WON A PET
SAVED BY LIFEGUARD
EMERGENCY ROOM VISIT
BROKE WINDOW
CALLED 911

■ SUBJECTS WHO DID NOT IMAGINE EVENT

▬ SUBJECTS WHO IMAGINED EVENT

0   20   40   60
PERCENT OF SUBJECTS WITH INCREASING CONFIDENCE THAT EVENT OCCURRED

BRYAN CHRISTIE

IMAGINING AN EVENT can increase a person's belief that the fictitious event actually happened. To study the "imagination inflation" effect, the author and her colleagues asked participants to indicate on a scale the likelihood that each of 40 events occurred during their childhood. Two weeks later they were given guidance in imagining some of the events they said had not taken place and then were asked to rate the original 40 events again. Whereas all participants showed increased confidence that the events had occurred, those who took part in actively imagining the events reported an even greater increase.

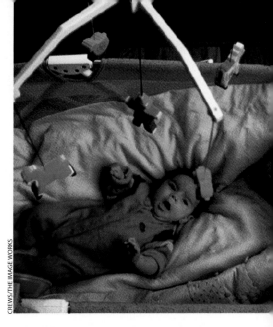

MEMORIES OF INFANCY—such as a mobile hanging over a crib—can be induced even though it is highly unlikely that events from the first year of life can be recalled. In a study by the late Nicholas Spanos and his colleagues at Carleton University, "impossible" memories of the first day of life were planted using either hypnosis or a guided mnemonic restructuring procedure. The mobile was "remembered" by 46 percent of the hypnotized group and by 56 percent of the guided group.

mobile did recall other things, such as doctors, nurses, bright lights, cribs and masks. Also, in both groups, of those who reported memories of infancy, 49 percent felt that they were real memories, as opposed to 16 percent who claimed that they were merely fantasies. These findings confirm earlier studies that many individuals can be led to construct complex, vivid and detailed false memories via a rather simple procedure. Hypnosis clearly is not necessary.

How False Memories Form

In the lost-in-the-mall study, implantation of false memory occurred when another person, usually a family member, claimed that the incident happened. Corroboration of an event by another person can be a powerful technique for instilling a false memory. In fact, merely claiming to have seen a person do something can lead that person to make a false confession of wrongdoing.

This effect was demonstrated in a study by Saul M. Kassin and his colleagues at Williams College, who investigated the reactions of individuals falsely accused of damaging a computer by pressing the wrong key. The innocent participants initially denied the charge, but when a confederate said that she had seen them perform the action, many participants signed a confession, internalized guilt for the act and went on to confabulate details that were consistent with that belief. These findings show that false

incriminating evidence can induce people to accept guilt for a crime they did not commit and even to develop memories to support their guilty feelings.

Research is beginning to give us an understanding of how false memories of complete, emotional and self-participatory experiences are created in adults. First, there are social demands on individuals to remember; for instance, researchers exert some pressure on participants in a study to come up with memories. Second, memory construction by imagining events can be explicitly encouraged when people are having trouble remembering. And, finally, individuals can be encouraged not to think about whether their constructions are real or not. Creation of false memories is most likely to occur when these external factors are present, whether in an experimental setting, in a therapeutic setting or during everyday activities.

False memories are constructed by combining actual memories with the content of suggestions received from others. During the process, individuals may forget the source of the information. This is a classic example of source confusion, in which the content and the source become dissociated.

Of course, because we can implant false childhood memories in some individuals in no way implies that all memories that arise after suggestion are necessarily false. Put another way, although experimental work on the creation of false memories may raise doubt about

the validity of long-buried memories, such as repeated trauma, it in no way disproves them. Without corroboration, there is little that can be done to help even the most experienced evaluator to differentiate true memories from ones that were suggestively planted.

The precise mechanisms by which such false memories are constructed await further research. We still have much to learn about the degree of confidence and the characteristics of false memories created in these ways, and we need to discover what types of individuals are particularly susceptible to these forms of suggestion and who is resistant.

As we continue this work, it is important to heed the cautionary tale in the data we have already obtained: mental health professionals and others must be aware of how greatly they can influence the recollection of events and of the urgent need for maintaining restraint in situations in which imagination is used as an aid in recovering presumably lost memories.

The Author

ELIZABETH F. LOFTUS is professor of psychology and adjunct professor of law at the University of Washington. She received her Ph.D. in psychology from Stanford University in 1970. Her research has focused on human memory, eyewitness testimony and courtroom procedure. Loftus has published 18 books and more than 250 scientific articles and has served as an expert witness or consultant in hundreds of trials, including the McMartin preschool molestation case. Her book *Eyewitness Testimony* won a National Media Award from the American Psychological Foundation. She has received honorary doctorates from Miami University, Leiden University and John Jay College of Criminal Justice. Loftus was recently elected president of the American Psychological Society.

Further Reading

THE MYTH OF REPRESSED MEMORY. Elizabeth F. Loftus and Katherine Ketcham. St. Martin's Press, 1994.
THE SOCIAL PSYCHOLOGY OF FALSE CONFESSIONS: COMPLIANCE, INTERNALIZATION, AND CONFABULATION. Saul M. Kassin and Katherine L. Kiechel in *Psychological Science*, Vol. 7, No. 3, pages 125–128; May 1996.
IMAGINATION INFLATION: IMAGINING A CHILDHOOD EVENT INFLATES CONFIDENCE THAT IT OCCURRED. Maryanne Garry, Charles G. Manning, Elizabeth F. Loftus and Steven J. Sherman in *Psychonomic Bulletin and Review*, Vol. 3, No. 2, pages 208–214; June 1996.
REMEMBERING OUR PAST: STUDIES IN AUTOBIOGRAPHICAL MEMORY. Edited by David C. Rubin. Cambridge University Press, 1996.
SEARCHING FOR MEMORY: THE BRAIN, THE MIND, AND THE PAST. Daniel L. Schacter. BasicBooks, 1996.

The "Visual Cliff"

This simple apparatus is used to investigate depth perception in different animals. All species thus far tested seem able to perceive and avoid a sharp drop as soon as they can move about

by Eleanor J. Gibson and Richard D. Walk

Human infants at the creeping and toddling stage are notoriously prone to falls from more or less high places. They must be kept from going over the brink by side panels on their cribs, gates on stairways and the vigilance of adults. As their muscular coordination matures they begin to avoid such accidents on their own. Common sense might suggest that the child learns to recognize falling-off places by experience—that is, by falling and hurting himself. But is experience really the teacher? Or is the ability to perceive and avoid a brink part of the child's original endowment?

Answers to these questions will throw light on the genesis of space perception in general. Height perception is a special case of distance perception: information in the light reaching the eye provides stimuli that can be utilized for the discrimination both of depth and of receding distance on the level. At what stage of development can an animal respond effectively to these stimuli? Does the onset of such response vary with animals of different species and habitats?

At Cornell University we have been investigating these problems by means of a simple experimental setup that we call a visual cliff. The cliff is a simulated one and hence makes it possible not only to control the optical and other stimuli (auditory and tactual, for instance) but also to protect the experimental subjects. It consists of a board laid across a large sheet of heavy glass which is supported a foot or more above the floor. On one side of the board a sheet of patterned material is placed flush against the undersurface of the glass, giving the glass the appearance as well as the substance of solidity. On the other side a sheet of the same material is laid upon the floor; this side of the board thus becomes the visual cliff [*see photograph on cover*].

We tested 36 infants ranging in age from six months to 14 months on the visual cliff. Each child was placed upon the center board, and his mother called him to her from the cliff side and the shallow side successively. All of the 27 infants who moved off the board crawled out on the shallow side at least once; only three of them crept off the brink onto the glass suspended above the pattern on the floor. Many of the infants crawled away from the mother when she called to them from the cliff side; others cried when she stood there, because they could not come to her without crossing an apparent chasm. The experiment thus demonstrated that most human infants can discriminate depth as soon as they can crawl.

The behavior of the children in this situation gave clear evidence of their dependence on vision. Often they would peer down through the glass on the deep side and then back away. Others would pat the glass with their hands, yet despite this tactual assurance of solidity would refuse to cross. It was equally clear that their perception of depth had matured more rapidly than had their locomotor abilities. Many supported themselves on the glass over the deep side as they maneuvered awkwardly on the board; some even backed out onto the glass as they started toward the mother on the shallow side. Were it not for the glass some of the children would have fallen off the board. Evidently infants should not be left close to a brink, no matter how well they may discriminate depth.

This experiment does not prove that the human infant's perception and avoidance of the cliff are innate. Such an interpretation is supported, however, by the experiments with nonhuman infants. On the visual cliff we have observed the behavior of chicks, turtles, rats, lambs, kids, pigs, kittens and dogs. These animals showed various reactions, each of which proved to be characteristic of their species. In each case the reaction is plainly related to the role of vision in the survival of the species, and the varied patterns of behavior suggest something about the role of vision in evolution.

In the chick, for example, depth perception manifests itself with special rapidity. At an age of less than 24 hours the chick can be tested on the visual cliff. It never makes a "mistake" and always hops off the board on the shallow side. Without doubt this finding is related to the fact that the chick, unlike many other young birds, must scratch for itself a few hours after it is hatched.

Kids and lambs, like chicks, can be tested on the visual cliff as soon as they can stand. The response of these animals is equally predictable. No goat or lamb ever stepped onto the glass of the deep side, even at one day of age. When one of these animals was placed upon the glass on the deep side, it displayed characteristic stereotyped behavior. It would refuse to put its feet down and would back up into a posture of defense, its front legs rigid and its hind legs limp. In this state of immobility it could be pushed forward across the glass until its head and field of vision crossed the edge of the surrounding solid surface, whereupon it would relax and spring forward upon the surface.

At the Cornell Behavior Farm a group of experimenters has carried these experiments with kids and goats a step further. They fixed the patterned material to a sheet of plywood and were thus able to adjust the "depth" of the deep side. With the pattern held immediately be-

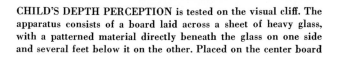

CHILD'S DEPTH PERCEPTION is tested on the visual cliff. The apparatus consists of a board laid across a sheet of heavy glass, with a patterned material directly beneath the glass on one side and several feet below it on the other. Placed on the center board (*top left*), the child crawls to its mother across the "shallow" side (*top right*). Called from the "deep" side, he pats the glass (*bottom left*), but despite this tactual evidence that the "cliff" is in fact a solid surface he refuses to cross over to the mother (*bottom right*).

neath the glass, the animal would move about the glass freely. With the optical floor dropped more than a foot below the glass, the animal would immediately freeze into its defensive posture. Despite repeated experience of the tactual solidity of the glass, the animals never learned to function without optical support. Their sense of security or danger continued to depend upon the visual cues that give them their perception of depth.

The rat, in contrast, does not depend predominantly upon visual cues. Its nocturnal habits lead it to seek food largely by smell, when moving about in the dark, it responds to tactual cues from the stiff whiskers (vibrissae) on its snout. Hooded rats tested on the visual cliff show little preference for the shallow side so long as they can feel the glass with their vibrissae. Placed upon the

KITTEN'S DEPTH PERCEPTION also manifests itself at an early age. Though the animal displays no alarm on the shallow side (*top*), it "freezes" when placed on the glass over the deep side (*bottom*); in some cases it will crawl aimlessly backward in a circle.

glass over the deep side, they move about normally. But when we raise the center board several inches, so that the glass is out of reach of their whiskers, they evince good visual depth-discrimination: 95 to 100 per cent of them descend on the shallow side.

Cats, like rats, are nocturnal animals, sensitive to tactual cues from their vibrissae. But the cat, as a predator, must rely more strongly on its sight. Kittens proved to have excellent depth-discrimination. At four weeks—about the earliest age that a kitten can move about with any facility—they invariably choose the shallow side of the cliff. On the glass over the deep side, they either freeze or circle aimlessly backward until they reach the center board [see illustrations on opposite page].

The animals that showed the poorest performance in our series were the turtles. The late Robert M. Yerkes of Harvard University found in 1904 that aquatic turtles have somewhat poorer depth-discrimination than land turtles. On the visual cliff one might expect an aquatic turtle to respond to the reflections from the glass as it might to water and so prefer the deep side. They showed no such preference: 76 per cent of the aquatic turtles crawled off the board on the shallow side. The relatively large minority that choose the deep side suggests either that this turtle has poorer depth-discrimination than other animals, or that its natural habitat gives it less occasion to "fear" a fall.

All of these observations square with what is known about the life history and ecological niche of each of the animals tested. The survival of a species requires that its members develop discrimination of depth by the time they take up independent locomotion, whether at one day (the chick and the goat), three to four weeks (the rat and the cat) or six to 10 months (the human infant). That such a vital capacity does not depend on possibly fatal accidents of learning in the lives of individuals is consistent with evolutionary theory.

To make sure that no hidden bias was concealed in the design of the visual cliff we conducted a number of control experiments. In one of them we eliminated reflections from the glass by lighting the patterned surfaces from below the glass (to accomplish this we dropped the pattern below the glass on both sides, but more on one side than on the other). The animals—hooded rats—still consistently chose the shallow side. As a test of the role of the patterned surface we

GOATS SHOW DEPTH PERCEPTION at an age of only one day. A kid walks freely on the shallow side (*top*); on the deep side (*middle*) it leaps the "chasm" to safety (*bottom*).

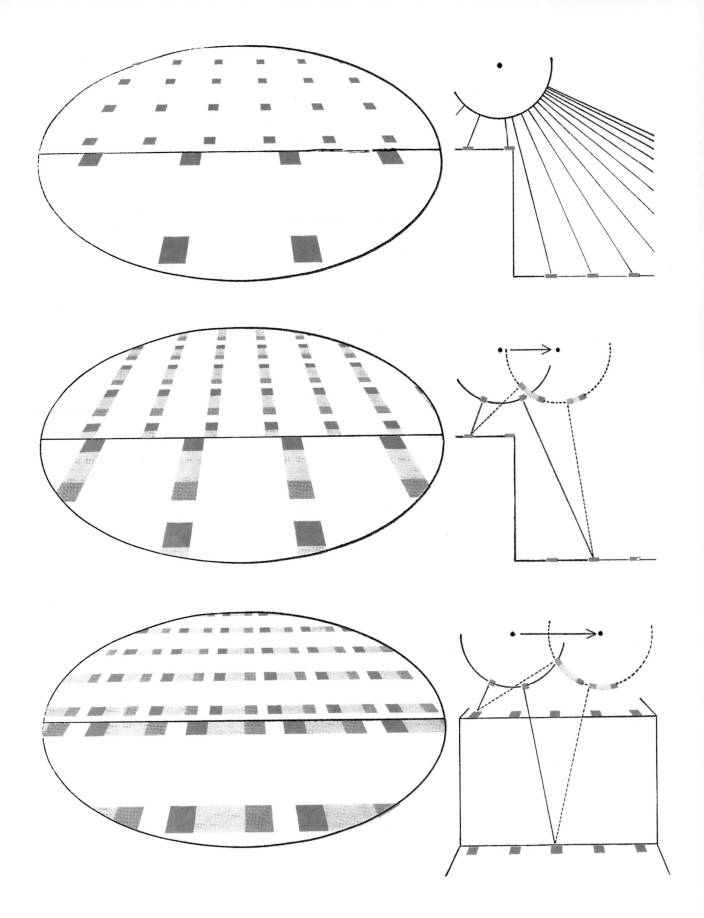

TWO TYPES OF VISUAL DEPTH-CUE are diagrammed schematically on this page. Ellipses approximate the visual field of an animal standing near the edge of the cliff and looking toward it; diagrams at right give the geometrical explanation of differences in the fields. The spacing of the pattern elements (*solid color*) decreases sharply beyond the edge of the cliff (*top*). The optical motion (*shaded color*) of the elements as the animal moves forward (*center*) or sideways (*bottom*) shows a similar drop-off.

replaced it on either side of the centerboard with a homogeneous gray surface. Confronted with this choice, the rats showed no preference for either the shallow or the deep side. We also eliminated the optical difference between the two sides of the board by placing the patterned surface directly against the undersurface of the glass on each side. The rats then descended without preference to either side. When we lowered the pattern 10 inches below the glass on each side, they stayed on the board.

We set out next to determine which of two visual cues plays the decisive role in depth perception. To an eye above the center board the optical pattern on the two sides differs in at least two important respects. On the deep side distance decreases the size and spacing of the pattern elements projected on the retina. "Motion parallax," on the other hand, causes the pattern elements on the shallow side to move more rapidly across the field of vision when the animal moves its position on the board or moves its head, just as nearby objects seen from a moving car appear to pass by more quickly than distant ones [see illustration on opposite page]. To eliminate the potential distance cue provided by pattern density we increased the size and spacing of the pattern elements on the deep side in proportion to its distance from the eye [see top illustration at right]. With only the cue of motion parallax to guide them, adult rats still preferred the shallow side, though not so strongly as in the standard experiment. Infant rats chose the shallow side nearly 100 per cent of the time under both conditions, as did day-old chicks. Evidently both species can discriminate depth by differential motion alone, with no aid from texture density and probably little help from other cues. The perception of distance by binocular parallax, which doubtless plays an important part in human behavior, would not seem to have a significant role, for example, in the depth perception of chicks and rats.

To eliminate the cue of motion parallax we placed the patterned material directly against the glass on either side of the board but used smaller and more densely spaced pattern-elements on the cliff side. Both young and adult hooded rats preferred the side with the larger pattern, which evidently "signified" a nearer surface. Day-old chicks, however, showed no preference for the larger pattern. It may be that learning plays some part in the preference exhibited by the

rats, since the young rats were tested at a somewhat older age than the chicks. This supposition is supported by the results of our experiments with animals reared in the dark.

The effects of early experience and of such deprivations as dark-rearing represent important clues to the relative roles of maturation and learning in animal behavior. The first experiments along this line were performed by K. S. Lashley and James T. Russell at the University of Chicago in 1934. They tested light-reared and dark-reared rats on a "jumping stand" from which they induced animals to leap toward a platform placed at varying distances. Upon finding that both groups of animals jumped with a force closely correlated with distance, they concluded that depth perception in rats is innate. Other investigators have pointed out, however, that the dark-reared rats required a certain amount of "pretraining" in the light before they could be made to jump. Since the visual-cliff technique requires no pretraining, we employed it to test groups of light-reared and dark-reared hooded rats. At the age of 90 days both groups showed the same preference for the shallow side of the apparatus, confirming Lashley's and Russell's conclusion.

Recalling our findings in the young rat, we then took up the question of whether the dark-reared rats relied upon motion parallax or upon contrast in texture density to discriminate depth. When the animals were confronted with the visual cliff, cued only by motion parallax, they preferred the shallow side, as had the light-reared animals. When the

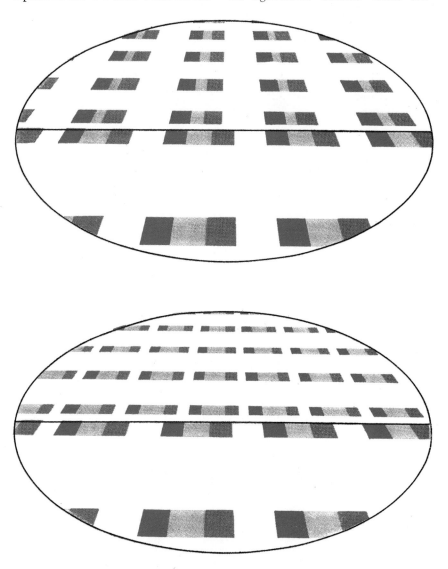

SEPARATION OF VISUAL CUES is shown in these diagrams. Pattern density is held constant (top) by using a larger pattern on the low side of the cliff; the drop in optical motion (motion parallax) remains. Motion parallax is equalized (bottom) by placing patterns at same level; the smaller pattern on one side preserves difference in spacing.

IMPORTANCE OF PATTERN in depth perception is shown in these photographs. Of two patterns set at the same depth, normal rats almost invariably preferred the larger (*top row and bottom left*), presumably because it "signified" a nearer and therefore safer surface. Confronted with two patternless surfaces set at different depths, the animals displayed no preference (*bottom right*).

choice was cued by pattern density, however, they departed from the pattern of the normal animals and showed no significant preference [see bottom illustration at right]. The behavior of dark-reared rats thus resembles that of the day-old chicks, which also lack visual experience. It seems likely, therefore, that of the two cues only motion parallax is an innate cue for depth discrimination. Responses to differential pattern-density may be learned later.

One cannot automatically extrapolate these results to other species. But experiments with dark-reared kittens indicate that in these animals, too, depth perception matures independently of trial and error learning. In the kitten, however, light is necessary for normal visual maturation. Kittens reared in the dark to the age of 27 days at first crawled or fell off the center board equally often on the deep and shallow sides. Placed upon the glass over the deep side, they did not back in a circle like normal kittens but showed the same behavior that they had exhibited on the shallow side. Other investigators have observed equivalent behavior in dark-reared kittens; they bump into obstacles, lack normal eye movement and appear to "stare" straight ahead. These difficulties pass after a few days in the light. We accordingly tested the kittens every day. By the end of a week they were performing in every respect like normal kittens. They showed the same unanimous preference for the shallow side. Placed upon the glass over the deep side, they balked and circled backward to a visually secure surface. Repeated descents to the deep side, and placement upon the glass during their "blind" period, had not taught them that the deep side was "safe." Instead they avoided it more and more consistently. The initial blindness of dark-reared kittens makes them ideal subjects for studying the maturation of depth perception. With further study it should be possible to determine which cues they respond to first and what kinds of visual experience accelerate or retard the process of maturation.

From our first few years of work with the visual cliff we are ready to venture the rather broad conclusion that a seeing animal will be able to discriminate depth when its locomotion is adequate, even when locomotion begins at birth. But many experiments remain to be done, especially on the role of different cues and on the effects of different kinds of early visual experience.

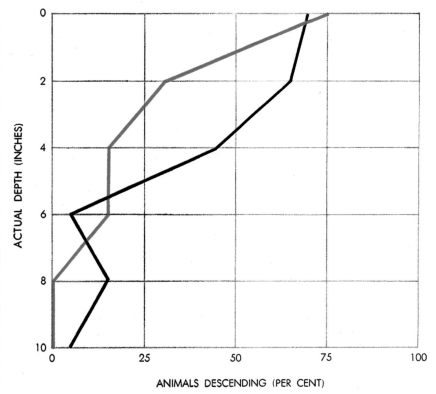

CONTROL EXPERIMENT measured the effect on rats of reflections on the glass of the apparatus. The percentage of animals leaving the center board decreased with increasing depth in much the same way, whether glass was present (*black curve*) or not (*colored curve*).

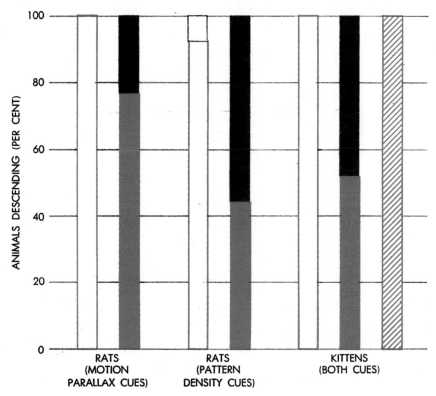

DARK-REARING EXPERIMENTS reveal the order in which different depth-cues are utilized as animals mature. Animals reared in the light (*open bars*) all strongly preferred the shallow side (*color*) to the deep side (*gray*). Dark-reared rats (*solid bars*), utilizing motion parallax alone, still preferred the shallow side; pattern density alone elicited no preference. Dark-reared kittens also showed no preference, because of temporary blindness. After seven days in the light all of them chose the shallow side (*hatched bar*).

Love in Infant Monkeys

Affection in infants was long thought to be generated by the satisfactions of feeding. Studies of young rhesus monkeys now indicate that love derives mainly from close bodily contact

by Harry F. Harlow

The first love of the human infant is for his mother. The tender intimacy of this attachment is such that it is sometimes regarded as a sacred or mystical force, an instinct incapable of analysis. No doubt such compunctions, along with the obvious obstacles in the way of objective study, have hampered experimental observation of the bonds between child and mother.

Though the data are thin, the theoretical literature on the subject is rich. Psychologists, sociologists and anthropologists commonly hold that the infant's love is learned through the association of the mother's face, body and other physical characteristics with the alleviation of internal biological tensions, particularly hunger and thirst. Traditional psychoanalysts have tended to emphasize the role of attaining and sucking at the breast as the basis for affectional development. Recently a number of child psychiatrists have questioned such simple explanations. Some argue that affectionate handling in the act of nursing is a variable of importance, whereas a few workers suggest that the composite activities of nursing, contact, clinging and even seeing and hearing work together to elicit the infant's love for his mother.

Now it is difficult, if not impossible, to use human infants as subjects for the studies necessary to break through the present speculative impasse. At birth the infant is so immature that he has little or no control over any motor system other than that involved in sucking. Furthermore, his physical maturation is so slow that by the time he can achieve precise, coordinated, measurable responses of his head, hands, feet and body, the nature and sequence of development have been hopelessly confounded and obscured. Clearly research into

the infant-mother relationship has need of a more suitable laboratory animal. We believe we have found it in the infant monkey. For the past several years our group at the Primate Laboratory of the University of Wisconsin has been employing baby rhesus monkeys in a study that we believe has begun to yield significant insights into the origin of the infant's love for his mother.

Baby monkeys are far better coordinated at birth than human infants. Their responses can be observed and evaluated with confidence at an age of 10 days or even earlier. Though they mature much more rapidly than their human contemporaries, infants of both species follow much the same general pattern of development.

Our interest in infant-monkey love grew out of a research program that involved the separation of monkeys from their mothers a few hours after birth. Employing techniques developed by Gertrude van Wagenen of Yale University, we had been rearing infant monkeys on the bottle with a mortality far less than that among monkeys nursed by their mothers. We were particularly careful to provide the infant monkeys with a folded gauze diaper on the floor of their cages, in accord with Dr. van Wagenen's observation that they would tend to maintain intimate contact with such soft, pliant surfaces, especially during nursing. We were impressed by the deep personal attachments that the monkeys formed for these diaper pads, and by the distress that they exhibited when the pads were briefly removed once a day for purposes of sanitation. The behavior of the infant monkeys was reminiscent of the human infant's attachment to its blankets, pillows, rag dolls or cuddly teddy bears.

These observations suggested the series of experiments in which we have sought to compare the importance of nursing and all associated activities with that of simple bodily contact in engendering the infant monkey's attachment to its mother. For this purpose we contrived two surrogate mother monkeys. One is a bare welded-wire cylindrical form surmounted by a wooden head with a crude face. In the other the welded wire is cushioned by a sheathing of terry cloth. We placed eight newborn monkeys in individual cages, each with equal access to a cloth and a wire mother [see *illustration on opposite page*]. Four of the infants received their milk from one mother and four from the other, the milk being furnished in each case by a nursing bottle, with its nipple protruding from the mother's "breast."

The two mothers quickly proved to be physiologically equivalent. The monkeys in the two groups drank the same amount of milk and gained weight at the same rate. But the two mothers proved to be by no means psychologically equivalent. Records made automatically showed that both groups of infants spent far more time climbing and clinging on their cloth-covered mothers than they did on their wire mothers. During the infants' first 14 days of life the floors of the cages were warmed by an electric heating pad, but most of the infants left the pad as soon as they could climb on the unheated cloth mother. Moreover, as the monkeys grew older, they tended to spend an increasing amount of time clinging and cuddling on her pliant terry-cloth surface. Those that secured their nourishment from the wire mother showed no tendency to spend more time on her than feeding required, contradicting the idea that affection is a response that is learned or derived in asso-

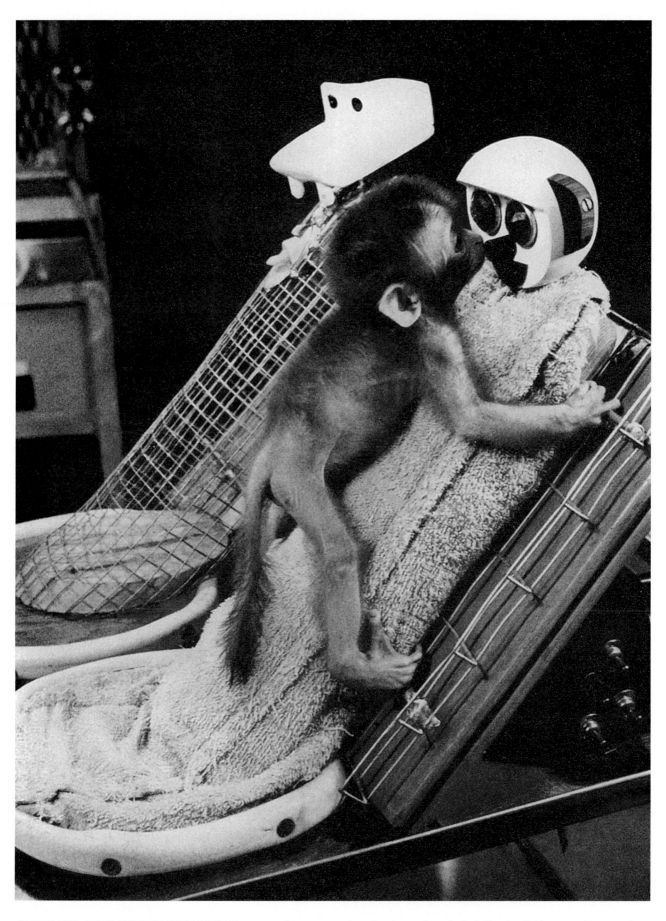

CLOTH AND WIRE MOTHER-SURROGATES were used to test the preferences of infant monkeys. The infants spent most of their time clinging to the soft cloth "mother," (*foreground*) even when nursing bottles were attached to the wire mother (*background*).

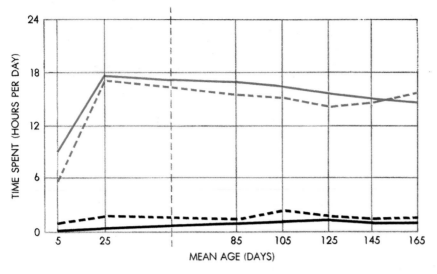

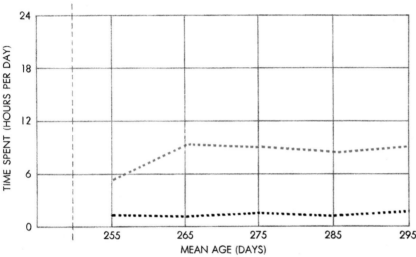

STRONG PREFERENCE FOR CLOTH MOTHER was shown by all infant monkeys. Infants reared with access to both mothers from birth (*top chart*) spent far more time on the cloth mother (*colored curves*) than on the wire mother (*black curves*). This was true regardless of whether they had been fed on the cloth (*solid lines*) or on the wire mother (*broken lines*). Infants that had known no mother during their first eight months (*bottom chart*) soon came to prefer cloth mother, but spent less time on her than the other infants.

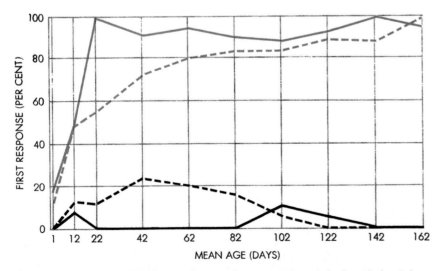

RESULTS OF "FEAR TEST" (*see photographs on opposite page*) showed that infants confronted by a strange object quickly learned to seek reassurance from the cloth mother (*colored curves*) rather than from the wire mother (*black curves*). Again infants fed on the wire mother (*broken lines*) behaved much like those fed on cloth mother (*solid lines*).

ciation with the reduction of hunger or thirst.

These results attest the importance—possibly the overwhelming importance—of bodily contact and the immediate comfort it supplies in forming the infant's attachment for its mother. All our experience, in fact, indicates that our cloth-covered mother surrogate is an eminently satisfactory mother. She is available 24 hours a day to satisfy her infant's overwhelming compulsion to seek bodily contact; she possesses infinite patience, never scolding her baby or biting it in anger. In these respects we regard her as superior to a living monkey mother, though monkey fathers would probably not endorse this opinion.

Of course this does not mean that nursing has no psychological importance. No act so effectively guarantees intimate bodily contact between mother and child. Furthermore, the mother who finds nursing a pleasant experience will probably be temperamentally inclined to give her infant plenty of handling and fondling. The real-life attachment of the infant to its mother is doubtless influenced by subtle multiple variables, contributed in part by the mother and in part by the child. We make no claim to having unraveled these in only two years of investigation. But no matter what evidence the future may disclose, our first experiments have shown that contact comfort is a decisive variable in this relationship.

Such generalization is powerfully supported by the results of the next phase of our investigation. The time that the infant monkeys spent cuddling on their surrogate mothers was a strong but perhaps not conclusive index of emotional attachment. Would they also seek the inanimate mother for comfort and security when they were subjected to emotional stress? With this question in mind we exposed our monkey infants to the stress of fear by presenting them with strange objects, for example a mechanical teddy bear which moved forward, beating a drum. Whether the infants had nursed from the wire or the cloth mother, they overwhelmingly sought succor from the cloth one; this differential in behavior was enhanced with the passage of time and the accrual of experience. Early in this series of experiments the terrified infant might rush blindly to the wire mother, but even if it did so it would soon abandon her for the cloth mother. The infant would cling to its cloth mother, rubbing its body against hers. Then, with its fears assuaged through intimate contact with the moth-

FRIGHTENING OBJECTS such as a mechanical teddy bear caused almost all infant monkeys to flee blindly to the cloth mother, as in the top photograph. Once reassured by pressing and rubbing against her, they would then look at the strange object (*bottom*).

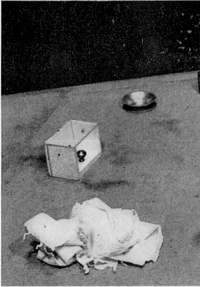

"OPEN FIELD TEST" involved placing a monkey in a room far larger than its accustomed cage; unfamiliar objects added an additional disturbing element. If no mother was present, the infant would typically huddle in a corner (*left*). The wire mother did

er, it would turn to look at the previously terrifying bear without the slightest sign of alarm. Indeed, the infant would sometimes even leave the protection of the mother and approach the object that a few minutes before had reduced it to abject terror.

The analogy with the behavior of human infants requires no elaboration. We found that the analogy extends even to less obviously stressful situations. When a child is taken to a strange place, he usually remains composed and happy so long as his mother is nearby. If the mother gets out of sight, however, the child is often seized with fear and distress. We developed the same response in our infant monkeys when we exposed them to a room that was far larger than the cages to which they were accustomed. In the room we had placed a number of unfamiliar objects such as a small artificial tree, a crumpled piece of paper, a folded gauze diaper, a wooden block and a doorknob [*a similar experiment is depicted in the illustrations on these two pages*]. If the cloth mother was in the room, the infant would rush wildly to her, climb upon her, rub against her and cling to her tightly. As in the previous experiment, its fear then sharply diminished or vanished. The infant would begin to climb over the mother's body and to explore and manipulate her face. Soon it would leave the mother to investigate the new world, and the unfamiliar objects would become playthings. In a typical behavior sequence, the infant might manipulate the tree, return to the mother, crumple the wad of paper, bring it to the mother, explore the block, ex-

plore the doorknob, play with the paper and return to the mother. So long as the mother provided a psychological "base of operations" the infants were unafraid and their behavior remained positive, exploratory and playful.

If the cloth mother was absent, however, the infants would rush across the test room and throw themselves facedown on the floor, clutching their heads and bodies and screaming their distress. Records kept by two independent observers—scoring for such "fear indices" as crying, crouching, rocking and thumb- and toe-sucking—showed that the emotionality scores of the infants nearly tripled. But no quantitative measurement can convey the contrast between the positive, outgoing activities in the presence of the cloth mother and the stereotyped withdrawn and disturbed behavior in the motherless situation.

The bare wire mother provided no more reassurance in this "open field" test than no mother at all. Control tests on monkeys that from birth had known only the wire mother revealed that even these infants showed no affection for her and obtained no comfort from her presence. Indeed, this group of animals exhibited the highest emotionality scores of all. Typically they would run to some wall or corner of the room, clasp their heads and bodies and rock convulsively back and forth. Such activities closely resemble the autistic behavior seen frequently among neglected children in and out of institutions.

In a final comparison of the cloth and wire mothers, we adapted an experiment originally devised by Robert A. Butler

at the Primate Laboratory. Butler had found that monkeys enclosed in a dimly lighted box would press a lever to open and reopen a window for hours on end for no reward other than the chance to look out. The rate of lever-pressing depended on what the monkeys saw through the opened window; the sight of another monkey elicited far more activity than that of a bowl of fruit or an empty room [see "Curiosity in Monkeys," by Robert A. Butler; SCIENTIFIC AMERICAN, February, 1954]. We now know that this "curiosity response" is innate. Three-day-old monkeys, barely able to walk, will crawl across the floor of the box to reach a lever which briefly opens the window; some press the lever hundreds of times within a few hours.

When we tested our monkey infants in the "Butler box," we found that those reared with both cloth and wire mothers showed as high a response to the cloth mother as to another monkey, but displayed no more interest in the wire mother than in an empty room. In this test, as in all the others, the monkeys fed on the wire mother behaved the same as those fed on the cloth mother. A control group raised with no mothers at all found the cloth mother no more interesting than the wire mother and neither as interesting as another monkey.

Thus all the objective tests we have been able to devise agree in showing that the infant monkey's relationship to its surrogate mother is a full one. Comparison with the behavior of infant monkeys raised by their real mothers confirms this view. Like our experimental monkeys, these infants spend many

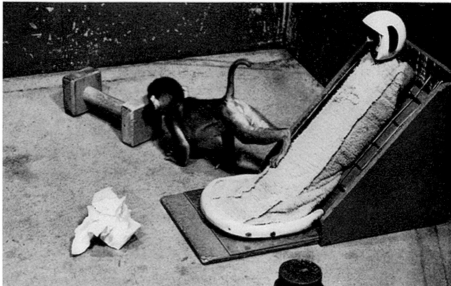

not alter this pattern of fearful behavior, but the cloth mother provided quick reassurance. The infant would first cling to her (*center*) and then set out to explore the room and play with the objects (*right*), returning from time to time for more reassurance.

hours a day clinging to their mothers, and run to them for comfort or reassurance when they are frightened. The deep and abiding bond between mother and child appears to be essentially the same, whether the mother is real or a cloth surrogate.

While bodily contact clearly plays the prime role in developing infantile affection, other types of stimulation presumably supplement its effects. We have therefore embarked on a search for these other factors. The activity of a live monkey mother, for example, provides her infant with frequent motion stimulation. In many human cultures mothers bind their babies to them when they go about their daily chores; in our own culture parents know very well that rocking a baby or walking with him somehow promotes his psychological and physiological well-being. Accordingly we compared the responsiveness of infant monkeys to two cloth mothers, one stationary and one rocking. All of them preferred the rocking mother, though the degree of preference varied considerably from day to day and from monkey to monkey. An experiment with a rocking crib and a stationary one gave similar results. Motion does appear to enhance affection, albeit far less significantly than simple contact.

The act of clinging, in itself, also seems to have a role in promoting psychological and physiological well-being. Even before we began our studies of affection, we noticed that a newborn monkey raised in a bare wire cage survived with difficulty unless we provided it with a cone to which it could cling. Re-

cently we have raised two groups of monkeys, one with a padded crib instead of a mother and the other with a cloth mother as well as a crib. Infants in the latter group actually spend more time on the crib than on the mother, probably because the steep incline of the mother's cloth surface makes her a less satisfactory sleeping platform. In the open-field test, the infants raised with a crib but no mother clearly derived some emotional support from the presence of the crib. But those raised with both showed an unequivocal preference for the mother they could cling to, and they evidenced the benefit of the superior emotional succor they gained from her.

Still other elements in the relationship remain to be investigated systematically. Common sense would suggest that the warmth of the mother's body plays its part in strengthening the infant's ties to her. Our own observations have not yet confirmed this hypothesis. Heating a cloth mother does not seem to increase her attractiveness to the infant monkey, and infants readily abandon a heating pad for an unheated mother surrogate. However, our laboratory is kept comfortably warm at all times; experiments in a chilly environment might well yield quite different results.

Visual stimulation may forge an additional link. When they are about three months old, the monkeys begin to observe and manipulate the head, face and eyes of their mother surrogates; human infants show the same sort of delayed responsiveness to visual stimuli. Such stimuli are known to have marked ef-

fects on the behavior of many young animals. The Austrian zoologist Konrad Lorenz has demonstrated a process called "imprinting"; he has shown that the young of some species of birds become attached to the first moving object they perceive, normally their mothers [see "'Imprinting' in Animals," by Eckhard H. Hess; SCIENTIFIC AMERICAN, March, 1958]. It is also possible that particular sounds and even odors may play some role in the normal development of responses or attention.

The depth and persistence of attachment to the mother depend not only on the kind of stimuli that the young animal receives but also on when it receives them. Experiments with ducks show that imprinting is most effective during a critical period soon after hatching; beyond a certain age it cannot take place at all. Clinical experience with human beings indicates that people who have been deprived of affection in infancy may have difficulty forming affectional ties in later life. From preliminary experiments with our monkeys we have found that their affectional responses develop, or fail to develop, according to a similar pattern.

Early in our investigation we had segregated four infant monkeys as a general control group, denying them physical contact either with a mother surrogate or with other monkeys. After about eight months we placed them in cages with access to both cloth and wire mothers. At first they were afraid of both surrogates, but within a few days they began to respond in much the same way as the other infants. Soon they were

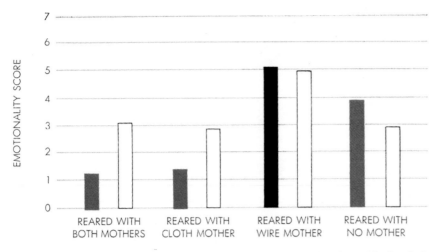

SCORES IN OPEN FIELD TEST show that all infant monkeys familiar with the cloth mother were much less disturbed when she was present (*color*) than when no mother was present (*white*); scores under 2 indicate unfrightened behavior. Infants that had known only the wire mother were greatly disturbed whether she was present (*black*) or not (*white*).

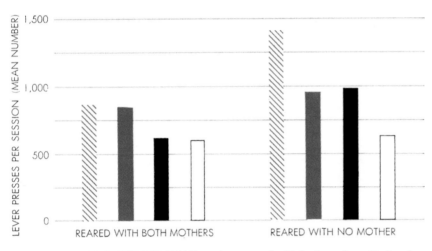

"CURIOSITY TEST" SHOWED THAT monkeys reared with both mothers displayed as much interest in the cloth mother (*solid color*) as in another monkey (*hatched color*); the wire mother (*black*) was no more interesting than an empty chamber (*white*). Monkeys reared with no mother found cloth and wire mother less interesting than another monkey.

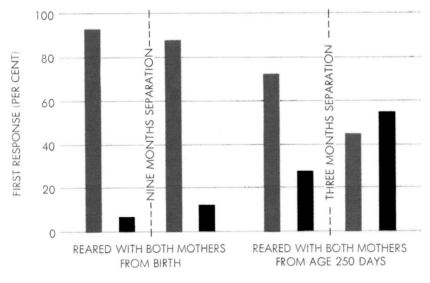

EARLY "MOTHERING" produced a strong and unchanging preference for the cloth mother (*color*) over the wire mother (*black*). Monkeys deprived of early mothering showed less marked preferences before separation and no significant preference subsequently.

spending less than an hour a day with the wire mother and eight to 10 hours with the cloth mother. Significantly, however, they spent little more than half as much time with the cloth mother as did infants raised with her from birth.

In the open-field test these "orphan" monkeys derived far less reassurance from the cloth mothers than did the other infants. The deprivation of physical contact during their first eight months had plainly affected the capacity of these infants to develop the full and normal pattern of affection. We found a further indication of the psychological damage wrought by early lack of mothering when we tested the degree to which infant monkeys retained their attachments to their mothers. Infants raised with a cloth mother from birth and separated from her at about five and a half months showed little or no loss of responsiveness even after 18 months of separation. In some cases it seemed that absence had made the heart grow fonder. The monkeys that had known a mother surrogate only after the age of eight months, however, rapidly lost whatever responsiveness they had acquired. The long period of maternal deprivation had evidently left them incapable of forming a lasting affectional tie.

The effects of maternal separation and deprivation in the human infant have scarcely been investigated, in spite of their implications concerning child-rearing practices. The long period of infant-maternal dependency in the monkey provides a real opportunity for investigating persisting disturbances produced by inconsistent or punishing mother surrogates.

Above and beyond demonstration of the surprising importance of contact comfort as a prime requisite in the formation of an infant's love for its mother —and the discovery of the unimportant or nonexistent role of the breast and act of nursing—our investigations have established a secure experimental approach to this realm of dramatic and subtle emotional relationships. The further exploitation of the broad field of research that now opens up depends merely upon the availability of infant monkeys. We expect to extend our researches by undertaking the study of the mother's (and even the father's!) love for the infant, using real monkey infants or infant surrogates. Finally, with such techniques established, there appears to be no reason why we cannot at some future time investigate the fundamental neurophysiological and biochemical variables underlying affection and love.

SCIENTIFIC AMERICAN

NOVEMBER, 1955   VOL. 193, NO. 5

Opinions and Social Pressure

*Exactly what is the effect of the opinions of others on our own?
In other words, how strong is the urge toward social conformity?
The question is approached by means of some unusual experiments*

by Solomon E. Asch

That social influences shape every person's practices, judgments and beliefs is a truism to which anyone will readily assent. A child masters his "native" dialect down to the finest nuances; a member of a tribe of cannibals accepts cannibalism as altogether fitting and proper. All the social sciences take their departure from the observation of the profound effects that groups exert on their members. For psychologists, group pressure upon the minds of individuals raises a host of questions they would like to investigate in detail.

How, and to what extent, do social forces constrain people's opinions and attitudes? This question is especially pertinent in our day. The same epoch that has witnessed the unprecedented technical extension of communication has also brought into existence the deliberate manipulation of opinion and the "engineering of consent." There are many good reasons why, as citizens and as scientists, we should be concerned with studying the ways in which human beings form their opinions and the role that social conditions play.

Studies of these questions began with the interest in hypnosis aroused by the French physician Jean Martin Charcot (a teacher of Sigmund Freud) toward the end of the 19th century. Charcot believed that only hysterical patients could be fully hypnotized, but this view was soon challenged by two other physicians, Hyppolyte Bernheim and A. A. Liébault, who demonstrated that they could put most people under the hypnotic spell. Bernheim proposed that hyp-nosis was but an extreme form of a normal psychological process which became known as "suggestibility." It was shown that monotonous reiteration of instructions could induce in normal persons in the waking state involuntary bodily changes such as swaying or rigidity of the arms, and sensations such as warmth and odor.

It was not long before social thinkers seized upon these discoveries as a basis for explaining numerous social phenomena, from the spread of opinion to the formation of crowds and the following of leaders. The sociologist Gabriel Tarde summed it all up in the aphorism: "Social man is a somnambulist."

When the new discipline of social psychology was born at the beginning of this century, its first experiments were

EXPERIMENT IS REPEATED in the Laboratory of Social Relations at Harvard University. Seven student subjects are asked by the experimenter (*right*) to compare the length of lines (*see diagram on the next page*). Six of the subjects have been coached beforehand to give unanimously wrong answers. The seventh (*sixth from the left*) has merely been told that it is an experiment in perception.

essentially adaptations of the suggestion demonstration. The technique generally followed a simple plan. The subjects, usually college students, were asked to give their opinions or preferences concerning various matters; some time later they were again asked to state their choices, but now they were also informed of the opinions held by authorities or large groups of their peers on the same matters. (Often the alleged consensus was fictitious.) Most of these studies had substantially the same result: confronted with opinions contrary to their own, many subjects apparently shifted their judgments in the direction of the views of the majorities or the experts. The late psychologist Edward L. Thorndike reported that he had succeeded in modifying the esthetic preferences of adults by this procedure. Other psychologists reported that people's evaluations of the merit of a literary passage could be raised or lowered by ascribing the passage to different authors. Apparently the sheer weight of numbers or authority sufficed to change opinions, even when no arguments for the opinions themselves were provided.

Now the very ease of success in these experiments arouses suspicion. Did the subjects actually change their opinions, or were the experimental victories scored only on paper? On grounds of common sense, one must question whether opinions are generally as watery as these studies indicate. There is some reason to wonder whether it was not the investigators who, in their enthusiasm for a theory, were suggestible, and whether the ostensibly gullible subjects were not providing answers which they thought good subjects were expected to give.

The investigations were guided by certain underlying assumptions, which today are common currency and account for much that is thought and said about the operations of propaganda and public opinion. The assumptions are that people submit uncritically and painlessly to external manipulation by suggestion or prestige, and that any given idea or value can be "sold" or "unsold" without reference to its merits. We should be skeptical, however, of the supposition that the power of social pressure necessarily implies uncritical submission to it: independence and the capacity to rise above group passion are also open to human beings. Further, one may question on psychological grounds whether it is possible as a rule to change a person's judgment of a situation or an object without first changing his knowledge or assumptions about it.

In what follows I shall describe some experiments in an investigation of the effects of group pressure which was carried out recently with the help of a number of my associates. The tests not only demonstrate the operations of group pressure upon individuals but also illustrate a new kind of attack on the problem and some of the more subtle questions that it raises.

A group of seven to nine young men, all college students, are assembled in a classroom for a "psychological experiment" in visual judgment. The experimenter informs them that they will be comparing the lengths of lines. He shows two large white cards. On one is a single vertical black line—the standard whose length is to be matched. On the other card are three vertical lines of various lengths. The subjects are to choose the one that is of the same length as the line on the other card. One of the three actually is of the same length; the other two are substantially different, the difference ranging from three quarters of an inch to an inch and three quarters.

The experiment opens uneventfully. The subjects announce their answers in the order in which they have been seated in the room, and on the first round every person chooses the same matching line.

Then a second set of cards is exposed; again the group is unanimous. The members appear ready to endure politely another boring experiment. On the third trial there is an unexpected disturbance. One person near the end of the group disagrees with all the others in his selection of the matching line. He looks surprised, indeed incredulous, about the disagreement. On the following trial he disagrees again, while the others remain unanimous in their choice. The dissenter becomes more and more worried and hesitant as the disagreement continues in succeeding trials; he may pause before announcing his answer and speak in a low voice, or he may smile in an embarrassed way.

What the dissenter does not know is that all the other members of the group were instructed by the experimenter beforehand to give incorrect answers in unanimity at certain points. The single individual who is not a party to this pre-arrangement is the focal subject of our experiment. He is placed in a position in which, while he is actually giving the correct answers, he finds himself unexpectedly in a minority of one, opposed by a unanimous and arbitrary majority with respect to a clear and simple fact. Upon him we have brought to bear two opposed forces: the evidence of his senses and the unanimous opinion of a group of his peers. Also, he must declare his judgments in public, before a majority which has also stated its position publicly.

The instructed majority occasionally reports correctly in order to reduce the possibility that the naive subject will suspect collusion against him. (In only a few cases did the subject actually show suspicion; when this happened, the experiment was stopped and the results were not counted.) There are 18 trials in each series, and on 12 of these the majority responds erroneously.

How do people respond to group pressure in this situation? I shall report first the statistical results of a series in which a total of 123 subjects from three institutions of higher learning (not including my own, Swarthmore College) were placed in the minority situation described above.

Two alternatives were open to the subject: he could act independently, repudiating the majority, or he could go along with the majority, repudiating the evidence of his senses. Of the 123 put to the test, a considerable percentage yielded to the majority. Whereas in ordinary circumstances individuals matching the lines will make mistakes less than 1

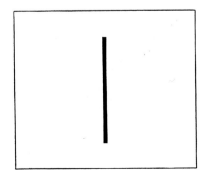 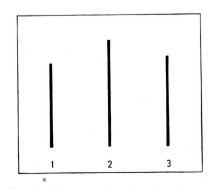

SUBJECTS WERE SHOWN two cards. One bore a standard line. The other bore three lines, one of which was the same length as the standard. The subjects were asked to choose this line.

per cent of the time, under group pressure the minority subjects swung to acceptance of the misleading majority's wrong judgments in 36.8 per cent of the selections.

Of course individuals differed in response. At one extreme, about one quarter of the subjects were completely independent and never agreed with the erroneous judgments of the majority. At the other extreme, some individuals went with the majority nearly all the time. The performances of individuals in this experiment tend to be highly consistent. Those who strike out on the path of independence do not, as a rule, succumb to the majority even over an extended series of trials, while those who choose the path of compliance are unable to free themselves as the ordeal is prolonged.

The reasons for the startling individual differences have not yet been investigated in detail. At this point we can only report some tentative generalizations from talks with the subjects, each of whom was interviewed at the end of the experiment. Among the independent individuals were many who held fast because of staunch confidence in their own judgment. The most significant fact about them was not absence of responsiveness to the majority but a capacity to recover from doubt and to reestablish their equilibrium. Others who acted independently came to believe that the majority was correct in its answers, but they continued their dissent on the simple ground that it was their obligation to call the play as they saw it.

Among the extremely yielding persons we found a group who quickly reached the conclusion: "I am wrong, they are right." Others yielded in order "not to spoil your results." Many of the individuals who went along suspected that the majority were "sheep" following the first responder, or that the majority were victims of an optical illusion; nevertheless, these suspicions failed to free them at the moment of decision. More disquieting were the reactions of subjects who construed their difference from the majority as a sign of some general deficiency in themselves, which at all costs they must hide. On this basis they desperately tried to merge with the majority, not realizing the longer-range consequences to themselves. All the yielding subjects underestimated the frequency with which they conformed.

Which aspect of the influence of a majority is more important—the size of the majority or its unanimity? The experiment was modified to examine this

EXPERIMENT PROCEEDS as follows. In the top picture the subject (*center*) hears rules of experiment for the first time. In the second picture he makes his first judgment of a pair of cards, disagreeing with the unanimous judgment of the others. In the third he leans forward to look at another pair of cards. In the fourth he shows the strain of repeatedly disagreeing with the majority. In the fifth, after 12 pairs of cards have been shown, he explains that "he has to call them as he sees them." This subject disagreed with the majority on all 12 trials. Seventy-five per cent of experimental subjects agree with the majority in varying degrees.

question. In one series the size of the opposition was varied from one to 15 persons. The results showed a clear trend. When a subject was confronted with only a single individual who contradicted his answers, he was swayed little: he continued to answer independently and correctly in nearly all trials. When the opposition was increased to two, the pressure became substantial: minority subjects now accepted the wrong answer 13.6 per cent of the time. Under the pressure of a majority of three, the subjects' errors jumped to 31.8 per cent. But further increases in the size of the majority apparently did not increase the weight of the pressure substantially. Clearly the size of the opposition is important only up to a point.

Disturbance of the majority's unanimity had a striking effect. In this experiment the subject was given the support of a truthful partner—either another individual who did not know of the prearranged agreement among the rest of the group, or a person who was instructed to give correct answers throughout.

The presence of a supporting partner depleted the majority of much of its power. Its pressure on the dissenting individual was reduced to one fourth: that is, subjects answered incorrectly only one fourth as often as under the pressure of a unanimous majority [see chart at lower left on the opposite page]. The weakest persons did not yield as readily. Most interesting were the reactions to the partner. Generally the feeling toward him was one of warmth and closeness; he was credited with inspiring confidence. However, the subjects repudiated the suggestion that the partner decided them to be independent.

Was the partner's effect a consequence of his dissent, or was it related to his accuracy? We now introduced into the experimental group a person who was instructed to dissent from the majority but also to disagree with the subject. In some experiments the majority was always to choose the worst of the comparison lines and the instructed dissenter to pick the line that was closer to the length of the standard one; in others the majority was consistently intermediate and the dissenter most in error. In this manner we were able to study the relative influence of "compromising" and "extremist" dissenters.

Again the results are clear. When a moderate dissenter is present, the effect of the majority on the subject decreases by approximately one third, and extremes of yielding disappear. Moreover, most of the errors the subjects do make are moderate, rather than flagrant. In short, the dissenter largely controls the choice of errors. To this extent the subjects broke away from the majority even while bending to it.

On the other hand, when the dissenter always chose the line that was more flagrantly different from the standard, the results were of quite a different kind. The extremist dissenter produced a remarkable freeing of the subjects; their errors dropped to only 9 per cent. Furthermore, all the errors were of the moderate variety. We were able to conclude that dissent per se increased independence and moderated the errors that occurred, and that the direction of dissent exerted consistent effects.

In all the foregoing experiments each subject was observed only in a single setting. We now turned to studying the effects upon a given individual of a change in the situation to which he was exposed. The first experiment examined the consequences of losing or gaining a partner. The instructed partner began by answering correctly on the first six trials. With his support the subject usually resisted pressure from the majority: 18 of 27 subjects were completely independent. But after six trials the partner joined the majority. As soon as he did so, there was an abrupt rise in the subjects' errors. Their submission to the majority was just about as frequent as when the minority subject was opposed by a unanimous majority throughout.

It was surprising to find that the experience of having had a partner and of having braved the majority opposition with him had failed to strengthen the individuals' independence. Questioning at the conclusion of the experiment suggested that we had overlooked an important circumstance; namely, the strong specific effect of "desertion" by the partner to the other side. We therefore changed the conditions so that the partner would simply leave the group at the proper point. (To allay suspicion it was announced in advance that he had an appointment with the dean.) In this form of the experiment, the partner's effect outlasted his presence. The errors increased after his departure, but less markedly than after a partner switched to the majority.

In a variant of this procedure the trials began with the majority unanimously giving correct answers. Then they gradually broke away until on the sixth trial the naive subject was alone and the group unanimously against him. As long as the subject had anyone on his side, he was almost invariably independent, but as soon as he found himself alone, the tendency to conform to the majority rose abruptly.

As might be expected, an individual's resistance to group pressure in these experiments depends to a considerable degree on how wrong the majority is. We varied the discrepancy between the standard line and the other lines systematically, with the hope of reaching a point where the error of the majority would be so glaring that every subject would repudiate it and choose independently. In this we regretfully did not succeed. Even when the difference between the lines was seven inches, there were still some who yielded to the error of the majority.

The study provides clear answers to a few relatively simple questions, and it raises many others that await investigation. We would like to know the degree of consistency of persons in situations which differ in content and structure. If consistency of independence or conformity in behavior is shown to be a fact, how is it functionally related to qualities of character and personality? In what ways is independence related to sociological or cultural conditions? Are leaders more independent than other people, or are they adept at following their followers? These and many other questions may perhaps be answerable by investigations of the type described here.

Life in society requires consensus as an indispensable condition. But consensus, to be productive, requires that each individual contribute independently out of his experience and insight. When consensus comes under the dominance of conformity, the social process is polluted and the individual at the same time surrenders the powers on which his functioning as a feeling and thinking being depends. That we have found the tendency to conformity in our society so strong that reasonably intelligent and well-meaning young people are willing to call white black is a matter of concern. It raises questions about our ways of education and about the values that guide our conduct.

Yet anyone inclined to draw too pessimistic conclusions from this report would do well to remind himself that the capacities for independence are not to be underestimated. He may also draw some consolation from a further observation: those who participated in this challenging experiment agreed nearly without exception that independence was preferable to conformity.

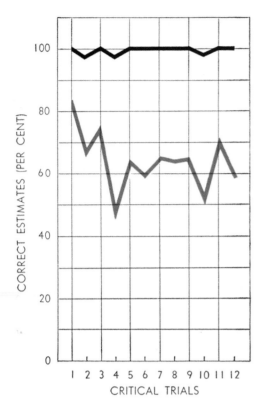

ERROR of 123 subjects, each of whom compared lines in the presence of six to eight opponents, is plotted in the colored curve. The accuracy of judgments not under pressure is indicated in black.

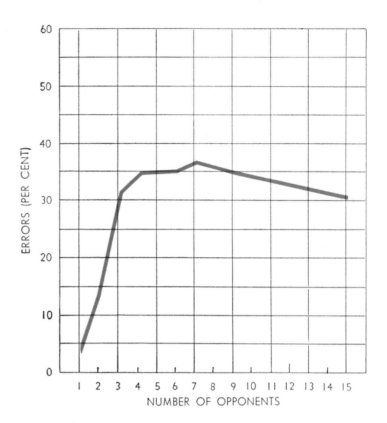

SIZE OF MAJORITY which opposed them had an effect on the subjects. With a single opponent the subject erred only 3.6 per cent of the time; with two opponents he erred 13.6 per cent; three, 31.8 per cent; four, 35.1 per cent; six, 35.2 per cent; seven, 37.1 per cent; nine, 35.1 per cent; 15, 31.2 per cent.

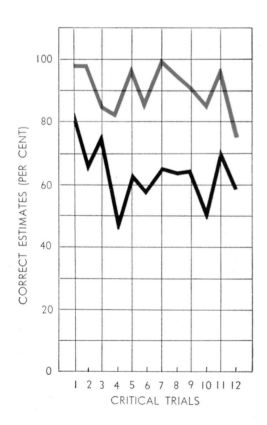

TWO SUBJECTS supporting each other against a majority made fewer errors (colored curve) than one subject did against a majority (black curve).

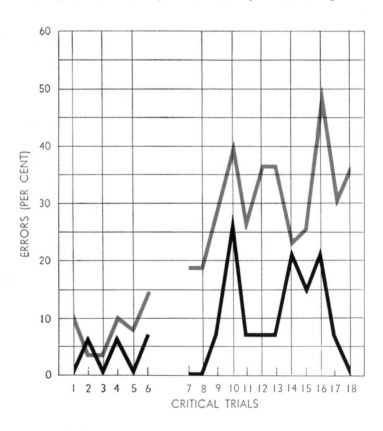

PARTNER LEFT SUBJECT after six trials in a single experiment. The colored curve shows the error of the subject when the partner "deserted" to the majority. Black curve shows error when partner merely left the room.